Toward an Effective Income Support System: Problems, Prospects, and Choices

with An Overview Paper

Toward an Effective Income Support System: Problems, Prospects, and Choices

Michael C. Barth
George J. Carcagno
John L. Palmer

with An Overview Paper

by
Irwin Garfinkel

Institute for Research on Poverty
University of Wisconsin–Madison

Toward an Effective Income Support System

Library of Congress Catalog Card Number: 74-6556

The Institute for Research on Poverty, University of Wisconsin-Madison 53706.

Printed in the United States of America.

Contents

List of Tables vii

Foreword ix

PART ONE

Introduction to the Paper 3
Toward an Effective Income Support System: Problems, Prospects, and Choices

Introduction 5

1 The Welfare System: Components, Characteristics, and Goals for Reform or Replacement 9

2 Programmatic Considerations and Options 47

3 The Work Requirement and Related Issues 60

4 Work-Conditioned Programs 71

5 Coverage of Intact Families 85

6 Coverage of the AFDC Population 92

7 Program Interrelationships 111

Summary and Conclusion 123

Appendix: Technical Characteristics of Income-Tested Transfer Programs 133

Notes to Part One 137

Glossary 146

PART TWO

Towards and Effective Income Support System: An Overview Paper 151

Notes to Part Two 167

Bibliography
Institute for Research on Poverty Publications Related to Welfare Policy Reform 171

General Publications Related to Welfare Policy Reform 179

Participants: Conference on Welfare Policy Reform 184

Index 187

List of Tables

1 The Social and Private Insurance System 13

2 Monthly Payment Standards in AFDC (Family of Four), July 1973 17

3 Average Medical Vendor Payments Per Family, Fiscal Year 1972 21

4 Number and Percentage Families with Incomes Below Poverty Level Before Transfers, and Number and Percentage Receiving Transfers, 1971 25

5 Extent of Poverty Alleviation by Social Insurance Programs 26

6 Antipoverty Effectiveness of Welfare Benefits (Cash Programs and Food Stamps) and Social Insurance Programs Combined 28

7 Types of Families Remaining Poor After Transfers 29

8 Average Family Size and Number of Individuals in Families Remaining Poor After Transfers 30

9	Reasons for Discontinuing Assistance of Female-Headed AFDC Cases	46
10	Estimated Income-Tested Portion, Social Transfers Account, Fiscal Year 1975	113

Foreword

Over the last several decades, both liberals and conservatives have objected to the nature of the nation's income support system and have called for its restructuring. In part as a response to these calls for "reform," the system has been continuously modified and extended, until today it bears little resemblance to that of 20 or 30 years ago.

The policy changes enacted, however, have not stilled the calls for reform and restructuring. Despite the modification and extension of the system, it is still seen by many as inequitable, demeaning, and inadequate. For many recipients, it erodes the incentives to work and encourages dependency on public subsidies. Moreover, the system is complex and disjointed and, because of that, it is administratively inefficient—indeed, wasteful.

The difficulties of satisfactorily restructuring a set of policies as complex as the nation's income support system are not hard to discern. They lie both within the very objectives that most people in the United States set for the system and within the differing weights that people attach to these objectives. They also inhere in the varying perceptions of the composition and the character of the primary group on which the system is targeted—the poor. The income support system, it is said, should provide "adequate" help, yet it should maintain and if possible strengthen work incentives. The structure of the system should recognize the many differences among potential beneficiaries, yet it should be comprehensive, simple to understand, and easy to administer. The system should not be stigmatizing or coercive, yet it should target the benefits on those most in need and ensure that those benefits purchase the goods and services required to satisfy the most basic human needs. The system should ensure that those families whose needs are the greatest receive the largest support, yet it should encourage beneficiaries to become independent of the system and self-sufficient. It is the tension among and, in some cases, the inconsistency of these desired characteristics that makes restructuring and reform so difficult to attain.

Less than five years ago, the last major federal legislative effort to restructure the income support system failed by a very small margin. Twice the Family Assistance Plan (FAP) passed the House of Representatives and at one point Senate passage seemed almost inevitable. Enactment of a single, comprehensive system of income support with national minimum income guarantees for all families, including the working poor, lacked only a few votes. Many reasons, sometimes conflicting, have been given for the legislative failure of FAP; this is not the place to review all of them. One important reason, however, is that the basic planning that underlay FAP gave insufficient attention to integrating the proposal with the several other income-tested support programs. While any fundamental reform proposal is likely to be viewed by some as destructive of work incentives and by others as inadequate, the lack of FAP's integration with other support programs gave substance to these views. Cumulative tax rates exceeding 100 percent, the accrual of benefits from several programs to individual families, and inconsistencies among programs in eligibility requirements, income definitions, and work requirements all indicated a disorganized and unwieldy system. FAP was viewed as exacerbating rather than correcting this problem.

Within a year after the failure of FAP, there was a new Presidential mandate to design a program that would fundamentally alter the income support system. The planning effort that was initiated assigned high priority to the objective of program rationalization and integration. Planners in the Department of Health, Education, and Welfare began to make a systematic study of the separate income transfer programs while attempting at the same time to view the system as a whole. One of the first results of this effort was a study paper prepared for an Administration Task Force on Welfare Reform. This paper described the nature of the current system, appraised its performance relative to several generally accepted norms, and evaluated proposed options for modification of the system with the help of these same norms. As such, the paper raised the full spectrum of issues that must be considered in designing any substantial improvement in the system and, given the norms posited, carefully analyzed the trade-offs among them implied by any proposed policy. In a very real sense, this paper was a primer on the nation's income transfer system; it presented a careful and reasoned discussion of virtually every issue that had been and would be raised in a "welfare reform" debate. It served as the basis for a series of subsequent Task Force papers that analyzed specific areas in depth.

In the summer of 1973, the Institute for Research on Poverty, in its role as consultant to the Department of Health, Education, and Welfare (and previously, the Office of Economic Opportunity) on research and analytic matters, was asked to review and critique an early draft of this study paper. The staff members of the Institute involved in the effort* were uniformly impressed with the paper as a thorough, objective, and comprehensive guide to the income transfer system. In its reliance on the results of basic research findings to enlighten policy issues, it was a model policy analysis. To researchers concerned with the ultimate policy impact of their analyses, a knowledgeable and accurate application of their own findings and those of other researchers was most gratifying.

In response to the Institute critique, the authors of the paper—Michael Barth, George Carcagno, and John Palmer—undertook a substantive revision of it. It was this revised version that served as the basic paper for the Task Force planning effort, and that is published in this volume. Its role in that effort is described by William Morrill in his "Introduction to the Paper."

In his State of the Union address in the early spring of 1974, the President suggested that these planning efforts would result in a major policy proposal by the Administration. Recognizing the complexity of the issue, he called for a long period of debate and discussion of the proposal and of the merits of the changes it

---

*The Institute staff participating in this review included: D. Lee Bawden, Glen Cain, Irwin Garfinkel, Joel Handler, Robert Haveman, Joe Heffernan, Jack Ladinsky, Robert Lampman, Charles Metcalf, Russell Middleton, Harold Watts, and Stanley Masters.

would entail. This volume is designed to contribute to and, hopefully, enlighten that debate; in at least three ways it serves this function.

First, as stated above, the HEW paper does raise and analyze the full range of issues on which any policy debate in this area should focus. It is felt that any citizen involved in this debate—Congressman, voter, or student—will benefit from this guide to the arguments on each side of each of the major issues. Any discussion of the problem following a reading of the paper will be a more informed discussion than that which would have occurred prior to its reading.

Second, it is enlightening to have in hand the planning paper that underlies whatever proposal the Administration ultimately submits. That proposal cannot help but be based upon and, to some extent, influenced by the analyses of the paper. Evaluation of that proposal will be aided by a full understanding of its underlying rationale.

Finally, included in this volume and following the HEW paper is an overview essay prepared by the Institute. This essay is based upon the participant discussion at a conference of experts held at the Institute for the purpose of discussing and appraising the paper and upon additional commentary and critique developed by Institute staff members. As such, it stands as a guide to and critique of the HEW paper and as an independent discussion of the implications of alternative approaches to modification of the nation's income support system. Sponsorship of the conference, and publication of the HEW paper and conference overview essay are consistent with the Institute's mandate to disseminate widely the results of its activities that contribute to an understanding of "the nature, causes, and cures of poverty."

Several members of the Institute staff should be singled out for special thanks for their efforts in arranging the conference and preparing the publication of this volume. Felicity Skidmore and Irwin Garfinkel were responsible for coordinating and scheduling the conference and arranging on short notice participation representing a broad spectrum of views. Beverly Neupert was of substantial help in ensuring that all of the many organizational matters required for a successful conference were attended to. Marjean Jondrow, Kitty Mochon, and Jean Mufti were crucial to the editing and production of the published documents. Their time and talents are reflected in both of the papers included in the volume. Finally, the typing of the several versions of the manuscripts was done with skill and cheer by Mary Sheean and by Julia Castro, Susan Elbe, Cathy Ersland, and Marlene Kundert.

Robert H. Haveman
Director
Institute for Research on Poverty

Part One

Toward an Effective Income Support System: Problems, Prospects, and Choices

Michael C. Barth
George J. Carcagno
John L. Palmer

Michael C. Barth is Director, Income Security Policy/Analysis in the Office of the Assistant Secretary for Planning and Evaluation, Office of the Secretary of Health, Eduation, and Welfare.

George J. Carcagno* is Vice President, Mathematica, Inc.

John L. Palmer is Director of Income Security Policy in the Office of the Assistant Secretary for Planning and Evaluation, Office of the Secretary of Health, Education, and Welfare.

This paper was prepared with the considerable assistance of Nancy Cole, Sandra Christensen, Frank Levy, Barbara Lindheim*, Janice Peskin, Naomi Salus, Charles Seagrave, John Todd, and Mark Worthington. With the exception of Ms. Lindheim and Mr. Levy, all are members of the Income Security Policy Staff. Ms. Christensen and Mr. Todd are Brookings Fellows on leave from the University of Maryland and Williams College, respectively. Mr. Levy is an associate professor of economics at the University of California, Berkeley. Ms. Lindheim is employed by Mathematica, Inc.

*The contributions to this paper by George J. Carcagno and Barbara Lindheim were performed pursuant to Contract (HEW-0S-73-192) with the Department of Health, Education, and Welfare.

Introduction to the Paper

by **William A. Morrill**—*Assistant Secretary for Planning and Evaluation, Department of Health, Education, and Welfare*

The reform of the Nation's income maintenance and related programs that comprise its welfare system has been and continues to be one of the more important domestic issues. In the aftermath of the enactment of a new Federally financed and administered program for the aged, blind, and disabled (the Supplementary Security Income program) and the second failure of the Family Assistance Program in the fall of 1972, the President expressed renewed interest in and determination to advance a thorough reform of the welfare system. His desire for a new proposal was expressed both publicly in his Human Resources Message of February 1973 and in his instructions to the new Secretary of Health, Education, and Welfare, Caspar W. Weinberger.

The Secretary initiated his assignment by establishing an interagency task force chaired by Under Secretary Frank Carlucci and requesting a review of the concerns involved in welfare reform. Leadership for the staff work was assigned to my office.

Against the background of an emotion-laden debate, yet unresolved, and with a largely new set of Executive branch actors with limited involvement in this debate, the first task—prior to development of specific alternative proposals—was to describe as objectively as possible the major issues and what could be said about them. The title paper of this book represents the effort to fulfill that task.

It is well to keep in mind the context in which the paper was produced, namely, a large department with busy leaders and an on-going set of both minor and major issues–welfare reform being but one of many in the latter category. As such the authors had the customary bureaucratic problem of what and how much to include in a document intended to be comprehensive, but also to be read. Balance had to be maintained between including all possible relevant information and exhausting the time and patience of busy executives. In addition, the document was not developed and used in a vacuum, but rather was surrounded with numerous discussion meetings with the department leadership for which separate work sheets, additional data, and the like were prepared.

We feel that the contribution of the document to the Task Force planning effort was an important one. The analysis of the paper served to effectively guide discussion toward those issues on which debate should focus and on which decisions had to be made, and away from irrelevancies and dead-ends. We believe it served the role that policy analysis should serve, and in an area in which conflicting objectives and program complexities abound.

With enough time and surely in light of the conference, the paper could usefully benefit from revision. Indeed, it received constructive criticism from its initial audience. It is, perhaps, just as useful to release it essentially in the form in which it was originally used as an illustration of the kind of staff work that is done on issues of this magnitude in the preliminary stages of proposal development.

I would like to acknowledge the contribution made by the Institute for Research on Poverty in making suggestions on an early draft, undertaking a conference on the document, and finally, in editing it for publication in this volume.

Introduction

Four years ago, President Nixon described the welfare system as a "colossal failure." "The tragedy," he said, "is not only that it is bringing states and cities to the brink of financial disaster, but also that it is failing to meet the elementary human, social, and financial needs of the poor."[1] Little has happened in the intervening period to dilute the force of that statement. The need to reform or replace the welfare system is still very much with us. What has happened in that period, however, is that our appreciation of the difficulty of designing an adequate reform proposal has been sharpened. The conflicting principles and goals of the welfare system have been revealed.

The series of publications by the Subcommittee on Fiscal Policy of the Joint Economic Committee, *Studies in Public Welfare,* has underscored the need for change.[2] These studies have brought out in sharp relief the inefficiencies, abuses, inequities, and unanticipated perverse results that mar the existing transfer system. The interaction between programs is also highlighted in the Committee's series. The inescapable conclusion is that a welfare system reform or replacement plan must be formulated within the context of all government transfer programs, including social insurance programs such as Unemployment Insurance and Social Security as well as those transfer programs explicitly designed to aid only the poor.

Any such new effort must overcome the legacy of both the

rhetoric that accompanied the earlier welfare reform debate and the legislative failure of the Family Assistance Plan (FAP). Nevertheless, the need to reform or replace a system that is an acknowledged failure must be dealt with. It is time to take a fresh look at the subject.

To reopen the issue does not in any way prejudge the result; it does not suggest that the major principles embodied in previous welfare reform attempts must be abandoned because they failed then to produce successful legislation. It does imply that all of the relevant alternatives should be considered, and that the arguments that lead to coming down on one or another side of a trade-off between inconsistent goals should be specified.

The purpose of this paper is to stimulate a dialogue on the issues of concern to all students of the welfare problem. This means examining questions ranging from, "Who should receive benefits?" to "How should two particular programs be related?" Thus, in large part this paper should serve as a heuristic device. It should help focus the attention of policymakers on the basic questions that need resolution. As the range of basic policy options at a general level (desired program coverage, for example) is narrowed, quantitative and analytical information on a specific set of options can be provided.

The remainder of this paper is divided into eight parts. Chapter 1 surveys the present income-tested transfer (welfare) system. After five of the principal components of that system—Aid to Families with Dependent Children (AFDC), food stamps, Medicaid, housing programs, and Supplementary Security Income (SSI)—are examined briefly, some data on the coverage of the transfer system will be presented. From this description some general problems emerge. Finally, some goals and criteria for policy in this area are noted. A supplement to Chapter 1 presents some new data on the dynamics of the poverty population, drawn from a five-year longitudinal survey and from studies on the welfare caseload.

Chapter 2 attempts to place past, present, and perhaps future welfare and welfare system reform or replacement programs in a clear framework. By examining first the simplest program type that meets a generally agreed upon set of policy goals and then, successively, program variants that were developed to meet specific policy concerns (like work effort), the trade-offs in welfare policy-making hopefully become evident. This chapter supplies descriptions of, and differentiates among, the major types of universal and categorical cash transfer programs. A brief opening section discusses the issues surrounding the form of a transfer: cash, voucher, or goods and services.

Chapter 3 discusses a range of issues surrounding the provision of transfers to those who are employed but earn very little or who are not employed but could in all probability work. Questions of work incentives, work requirements, employability, availability of employment, manpower services, and public employment are examined, and present knowledge in these areas summarized.

Chapter 4 describes a number of work-conditioned income transfer programs that have recently received a good deal of attention from those who wish to tie closely transfer benefits to work effort. In so doing, it lays out the programmatic options available to meet certain of the concerns discussed in Chapter 3. In addition, this chapter along with Chapter 2 supplies a reasonably complete description of the major transfer programs.

Under the existing transfer system a significant population group is largely left out–intact families with children, particularly those with a working head. Chapter 5 attempts to clarify the programmatic issues involved in covering this population and also suggests what sort of programs could be developed to cover non-AFDC families.

Chapter 6 examines the various ways in which the present AFDC program could be made more efficient and equitable. Many of the possible modifications in that program are already under serious consideration by the Department of Health, Education, and Welfare (DHEW), and it is important to clarify how such actions fit within a broader welfare system reform or replacement policy.

Chapter 7 examines the crucial issues that as a group have come to be known as problems in "program interrelation." That is, in a world with a variety of programs attempting to meet both similar and different needs of different populations, some overlap and undesirable interaction is inevitable. It appears that a great deal of the so-called "welfare mess" arises from just such overlap and interaction. This part first posits a holistic view of the system that yields some rather obvious but nonetheless important (and heretofore largely unheeded) suggestions for program coordination. This is followed by a brief discussion of the various techniques by which two or more programs, or the whole system, can be sensibly related.

The Summary and Conclusions section, which follows, should help the reader to focus on many of the important issues dealt with in the body of the paper and to define the important questions that must be debated as the process leading to the development of a specific proposal continues. The Appendix describes the common characteristics of income-tested transfer programs. It is followed by a glossary of terms used in the paper.

1

The Welfare System: Components, Characteristics, and Goals for Reform or Replacement

This part of the paper is intended to serve three purposes. First, the various means by which our society attempts to meet the consumption needs of its citizens are described in a broad and general way. The appropriate role of a welfare system and its interrelatedness with other systems providing for consumption needs should become apparent. Second, the nature and functioning of our present welfare system, particularly its inadequacies, are described. An understanding of these factors facilitates the development of a specific set of criteria that an income-tested cash transfer system should satisfy. Third, some criteria to serve as a guide for the discussion of the possible structural reforms, which occupies the remainder of the paper, are identified. In a supplement to this section of the paper some data, only recently available, on the dynamic nature of both the Aid to Families with Dependent Children (AFDC) and poverty populations and a brief discussion of their policy implications are included.

Employment, Social Insurance, and Welfare Policies

The following framework, although admittedly an oversimplification, provides a point of departure for the subsequent discussions of the welfare system.

Over time our society has evolved three systems and a related set of public policies upon which it largely depends for the provision of consumption needs:[3] the employment system, the social and private insurance system, and the welfare system.

- The employment system provides opportunities for remunerative work in both the private and public sectors. Ideally, ablebodied workers would be able to support themselves and their families entirely on earned income during their periods of employment.

- The social and private insurance system provides income protection for workers and their families, primarily by replacing a portion of earnings that are discontinued due to unemployment, disability, retirement, or death. Ideally, workers and their families would be ensured a standard of living not too far below that maintained before their earnings were disrupted.

- The welfare system is intended to provide some minimum standard of adequacy of consumption for some persons who, for various reasons, are not receiving sufficient income from other sources. Not all families with insufficient incomes are covered by the welfare system. Although private charities and other institutions participate in this system, it is dominated by the public sector.

Further elaboration on these three systems and the public policies that affect them should make possible a better understanding of the role of welfare and its relation to the other two systems and to relevant public policies.

EMPLOYMENT POLICY

Employment policy and the problems that our social insurance and welfare systems are designed to address are closely interrelated, a factor that cannot be overemphasized. Consider the following:

- In our society, it is generally regarded as more desirable to increase income in the form of earnings, or transfers that are related to past earnings, than in the form of welfare cash payments. The basic idea that income should be earned, if possible, is not likely to be altered, though, in time, our basic definition of work may change.

- Generally speaking, greater employment means greater economic growth and less need for welfare programs to provide for minimum standards of adequate consumption.

- As the unemployment rate decreases, lower income groups show relatively greater increases in earned income because low-income workers are usually at the end of the hiring queue. The only significant, lasting shift in the income distribution that has taken place in this country in the twentieth century occurred during World War II, when the unemployment rate was consistently below the levels that prevailed both before and after the war. Of course, many other factors were at work during that period: strong wage and price controls, very high manpower needs of the military, cost-plus contracts, and other such modifying elements. The shift in income distribution became permanent partly because of the large numbers of formerly very low wage, disadvantaged workers who received considerable on-the-job training and work experience during this period, and thus came to earn higher wages.

- The fewer the employment opportunities, the greater the burden on both the social and private insurance and welfare systems. The higher the levels of employment our nation can sustain, the more employment-related insurance can be relied on to carry us through relatively slack periods (both in the aggregate and in individual instances) and the less the welfare system need be relied on for any but those who have no current or previous attachment to the labor force.

- High unemployment tends to make welfare programs more complex and difficult to administer. The higher the unemployment rate, the greater the need for special measures to promote employment possibilities for welfare recipients. There is an increasing belief among some policymakers that these measures may have to include the creation of a considerable number of jobs.

The above considerations suggest that the government should place heavy emphasis on measures to increase aggregate demand and on education and manpower policies (including equal employment opportunity policies) designed to minimize and distribute more evenly any existing burden of unemployment. However, we are presently being acutely reminded of the limitations of the former, and the evidence is that the latter cannot be expected to have as major an impact as might previously have been hoped. (The role of manpower services in welfare policy is discussed further in Chapter 3.)

SOCIAL AND PRIVATE INSURANCE POLICY

The primary function of employment-related social and private insurance is to replace potential earnings lost due to unemployment, disability, retirement, or death. This represents society's backup system to ease the hardships caused by an abrupt cessation of earned income. An effective national employment policy enhances the role of this system in the overall income support system because as more individuals have a closer attachment to the labor force, more are eligible for work-related insurance, and fewer require welfare assistance when their earnings are disrupted.

An outline of the public and private programs that together comprise this system is provided in Table 1.

Both the private and public components of this system are in need of considerable strengthening. The coverage is generally inadequate. Some actions are currently under consideration in Congress—for example, federal minimum standards for the Unemployment Insurance system and various approaches to private pension reform. In addition, the Workmen's Compensation system is now under scrutiny. In general, however, insufficient attention has been paid to this system, in part because the analytic issues involved are extremely difficult.

Perhaps the most perplexing problems are presented by disability coverage, which is particularly inadequate and is also under study. As much as 25 percent of the poverty population is in households headed by a person who is "disabled," when disability is broadly defined. If disability coverage were strengthened in the social and private insurance system, a considerable

TABLE 1: THE SOCIAL AND PRIVATE INSURANCE SYSTEM

REASON FOR EARNINGS LOSS	EARNINGS REPLACEMENT PROGRAM
Temporary unemployment	Unemployment Insurance (UI)
Disability	
Resulting from work, total and partial	Workmen's Compensation (WC) Veteran's Compensation
Not resulting from work	Sick leave (provided by public and private employers)
Short term	Temporary Disability Insurance (TDI) (both public and private)
Long term, total	Social Security (OASDI) Long-term disability insurance, Early retirement pensions
Retirement	
Low- to middle-income retirees	Social Security (OASDI) Some private provision (pensions, annuities)
Middle- to upper-income retirees	Social Security (OASDI) Considerable private provision
Death	Life Insurance Social Security

burden could be taken off the welfare system.

In addition, it should be noted that many features have been introduced into the social insurance system that are not strictly related to its earnings-replacement function, but serve more of a welfare function. Such items include the legislatively mandated minimum benefit levels in both UI and OASDI and the considerable "loosening" of eligibility criteria.

WELFARE POLICY

If full employment could be maintained and education and manpower policies were sufficient to provide adequate incomes to all families with an ablebodied head, and if the earnings replacement of our social and private assistance programs were adequate, then welfare would only be concerned with families in which no one is currently employable and with families in which there was no eligibility for social insurance programs.

However, such is not the case. Our country's employment system and work-related insurance programs do not provide sufficient earning potential and income replacement to allow all those with a significant attachment to the labor force to avoid poverty. Thus, in addition to the need for substantial income assistance for those in families without labor force participants, there is a need for assistance to families with persons who are employable but are underemployed or unemployed, as well as some special manpower and employment policies so that they might become less dependent. Many people working full time, or nearly full time, are still not able to earn enough to keep themselves or their families out of poverty. They require regular, but small, supplementation in order to raise their incomes to minimum standards of adequacy.

The role of the welfare system has been defined above. Before the extent to which the present system is fulfilling this role can be determined, that system must be examined. This paper, while explicitly addressing ways of better integrating income-tested (welfare) and non-income-tested(social insurance) programs, focuses primarily on income-tested cash and noncash programs in the welfare system.

The Components of the Welfare System

The present transfer system is not, in fact, a system as traditionally defined, with rationally interacting elements that are mutually reinforcing. Rather, it consists of numerous programs with different goals and other characteristics, not an unexpected situation since each component was independently developed. However, this program mix has generated two unforeseen results. First, interactions between programs often produce undesirable effects. For example, in many of these programs, benefits are reduced as the recipient's earnings rise. While no single benefit reduction rate may seem excessive, the cumulative effect for an individual receiving benefits from several programs may be an implicit benefit reduction rate[4] of more than 100 percent. Second, both the benefit levels and scope of coverage of the programs are inadequate and inefficient in terms of their anti-poverty impact, despite the high cost.[5] These points are elaborated on below.

All income-tested programs, by definition, provide benefits only to persons whose incomes are below some eligibility level. In addition, to receive cash assistance the individual must be aged, blind, or permanently and totally disabled (SSI); or in the case of a family with children, have lost the support of a parent through death, incapacity, or absence of a parent from the home (AFDC); or in some states, because of unemployment of the father (AFDC-UF). Eligibility for the noncash programs is generally automatic for recipients of cash assistance, but coverage often goes beyond that population.

In the welfare system, there are five major component programs: Aid to Families with Dependent Children, food stamps, Medicaid, housing, and Supplemental Security Income.

AID TO FAMILIES WITH DEPENDENT CHILDREN

AFDC is the largest, most costly, and most controversial component of public assistance. It is estimated that in 1973 total benefits of $7.8 billion will have been paid to 12.6 million persons in 3.4 million families. The federal share of costs will have been about $4.3 billion, or 55 percent of the total.

The objective of AFDC, as defined in the Social Security Act, is

> to enable each state to furnish financial assistance, rehabilitation, and other services in order to encourage the care of dependent children in their own homes or in the homes of relatives with whom they are living, to help such parents or relatives to attain or retain the capability for self-support, and to help maintain and strengthen family life.

Eligibility for AFDC is thus based on more than financial need. Payments are made only to certain categories of families: those in which there is a dependent child who has been deprived of parental support or care by reason of death, continued absence from home, or physical or mental incapacity of a parent. Payments to two-parent families are the exception rather than the rule, even in the 23 states that have elected to pay AFDC-UF (unemployed father) benefits. In February 1973, only 5 percent of the nation's total AFDC recipients were enrolled in AFDC-UF.[6]

The relatively small number of persons covered by the AFDC-UF program is readily explained by the eligibility requirements for the program. A family is eligible only when the following conditions are met: the father has been unemployed (working less than 100 hours per month) for at least 30 consecutive days, has not (without good cause) refused a bona fide offer of employment or training, has six or more quarters of work in any 13-calendar-quarter period ending within one year of the application for benefits, is registered with the State Employment Service, and is not eligible to receive unemployment compensation. The exclusion of UI eligibles and recent labor force entrants drastically limits the eligible population, without regard to the economic need of the excluded persons. The 100-hour-per-month work limitation means that an AFDC-UF recipient becomes ineligible if he works more than the limit, without regard to his income level. Thus, an additional hour of work can result in the full loss of benefits.

Each of the 54 welfare jurisdictions participating in the AFDC program is required by law to establish a single agency to administer the program.[7] This, in effect, merely defines the agency that deals directly with the federal government for the purposes of administration and financial matters. The single agencies may, in turn, delegate direct administrative responsibility to lower levels of government. As a result, there is great variation among the states in the organizational units that administer AFDC. Twenty-two states delegate administration of the program to local government, generally the county level. States using that administrative model usually require that the local government unit shares in the costs of the program. Twenty-eight states have welfare programs administered solely by the state agency.

The wide range of administrative structures inevitably results in a wide range of administrative practices. In addition, since many of the basic program parameters are left to the discretion of the states, there are large variations in key program characteristics. For example, benefit levels vary widely among states: Average monthly AFDC benefits per recipient in April 1973 were $82.71 in New York and $14.40 in Mississippi. Differences in payment standards for the fifty states are shown in Table 2. While some differential would be necessary to allow for variations in the cost of living between regions, the difference of $68 per month between New York and Mississippi is too great to be attributed to this reason. Intrastate differences in the cost of living are as great as interstate. Lessening these differentials through federal programs, however, would entail real disadvantages in the eyes of those who view income maintenance as a local responsibility. The issue of which level of government should take primary responsibility for the design and administration of the welfare system is addressed below. For the moment, however, consider how the individual recipient relates to AFDC.

TABLE 2: MONTHLY PAYMENT STANDARDS IN AFDC (FAMILY OF FOUR), JULY 1973

	Payment Standard	*Largest Amount Paid**		*Payment Standard*	*Largest Amount Paid**
Alabama	$104	$ –	Missouri	$377	$158
Alaska	400	375	Montana	223	–
Arizona	282	184	Nebraska	307	226
Arkansas	275	130	Nevada	329	201
California	322	290	New Hampshire	294	–
Colorado	242	–	New Jersey	324	–
Connecticut	311	–	New Mexico	203	191
Delaware	287	152	New York	380	354
District of Columbia	246	–	North Carolina	184	–
			North Dakota	300	–
Florida	223	151	Ohio	258	200
Georgia	227	160	Oklahoma	226	192
Hawaii	385	–	Oregon	354	328
Idaho	251	–	Pennsylvania	313	–
Illinois	279	–	Rhode Island	263	–
Indiana	363	205	South Carolina	217	108
Iowa	341	243	South Dakota	310	–
Kansas	322	–	Tennessee	217	132
Kentucky	234	171	Texas	187	140
Louisiana	110	–	Utah	332	256
Maine	349	168	Vermont	335	–
Maryland	200	–	Virginia	279	261
Massachusetts	358	–	Washington	321	–
Michigan	372	364	West Virginia**	138	–
Minnesota	339	–	Wisconsin	312	302
Mississippi	277	60	Wyoming	260	–

** If different than the payment standard.*
*** 1971 data.*

Each state establishes a basic needs standard. An applicant's income is compared to the needs standard to determine eligibility. If income is below the needs standard, the family is eligible for AFDC. In some states, the needs standard is exceedingly complex, for it takes into account the individual needs of each family at a level of detail that is staggering. Does the family have to travel to do its laundry? If so, a mileage allowance may be included in the grant. Does the family have term life insurance? If so, the premiums may be paid. Is there a telephone? If so, the basic monthly rate may be added to the grant. The result is a system that rests on the subjective decisions of case workers and that, as a consequence, is subject to many questionable variations and errors.[8]

Once eligibility is established, the benefit is calculated. If the family has no income, the benefit equals all or a fraction of the needs standard.[9] If the family receives unearned income, it is applied dollar for dollar against the needs standard in most cases. If the family head is employed, $30 plus one-third of monthly earnings, plus an allowance for work-related expenses, such as day care, transportation costs, and uniforms, are retained by the recipient. While this indicates that welfare recipients may face a statutory marginal tax rate or benefit reduction rate of 67 percent on earnings, the benefit reduction rate can be even higher, since other programs providing benefits to AFDC families also have tax rates that reduce benefits as income rises. That is, benefit reduction rates cumulate.

On the other hand, the $30 disregard and the allowance in the AFDC program for work-related expenses mean that the average (effective) benefit reduction rate is lower than 67 percent. Each state determines how work-related expenses are treated. All states reimburse mandatory payroll deductions: income taxes, payroll taxes, and union dues, for example. Within states, different welfare districts may have different policies on work expenses. In actual practice, there are differences in the way individual social workers handle these expenses. There is, in fact, a good deal of evidence that suggests that effective benefit reduction rates under AFDC are well below 67 percent in some places because of the liberal disregarding of work-related expenses.[10] Therefore, any change in the system that would bring effective tax rates close to 67 percent would reduce the work incentives for some persons and, perhaps, improve them for others.

It should be noted that the average benefit reduction rates vary greatly between and within welfare jurisdictions. Social workers may act in individual cases in a way that minimizes the disincentive effects of high benefit reduction rates; this means that the policies concerning the preservation and promotion of work incentives are left to the essentially unguided discretion of persons at the non-policy-making level of the system.

In addition to the incentive structure described above, the AFDC program has work requirements for employable recipients. Such persons must register with the State Employment Service for work or training. Work requirements impose certain conditions on the system. First, if not enough jobs are available or provided through some mechanism such as public service employment, a rationing device must be developed. Second, day care should be provided and again rationing may be necessary. Third, the administration of the program is made more complex because of the need to make determinations on who is and who is not employable, whether employables have received offers of suitable employment, what job or training is suitable, and other such criteria.

The Work Incentives Program (WIN) is the primary vehicle for the delivery of manpower services to AFDC recipients. Administered by State Employment Services, the program has undergone various changes designed to make it more effective. Evaluations of the program to date indicate that it has not been very successful in increasing the earning potential of the participants. The WIN program is discussed in greater detail in Chapter 3.

FOOD STAMPS

The goal of the food stamp program as expressed by Congress is to improve the diets of low-income households and to expand the market for domestically produced food. Administered at the federal level by the Department of Agriculture, the program is operated by state and local welfare offices. Open-ended federal appropriations fully support program benefits while administrative costs are shared. It is estimated that in Fiscal Year 1973 (FY 73), total benefits (that is, the bonus value of food stamps, as defined below) to 13.2 million persons will have been on the order of $2.2 billion.

All AFDC households are automatically eligible for food stamps[11] while the eligibility of non-public-assistance households depends on family income, family size, and the value of certain assets. Eligible families may purchase coupons and use them like cash for most food items.

The price of food stamps to a given family varies with income, while the face value of the total amount of the food stamps a participating family can purchase varies with family size. Thus, the bonus value, or food stamp benefit—food stamp face value minus its purchase price—varies with family size and income.

A rise in family income results in a reduction of the food stamp bonus. While there is some slight variation, for most families the purchase price rises about $3 for each $10 increase in net income—a 30 percent benefit reduction rate. As with AFDC, the average benefit reduction is lower since taxes and other expenses are disregarded when determining income for the calculation of benefits.

Thus, a food stamp recipient family that participates in only that program faces a benefit reduction rate of about 30 percent as earnings rise. If a recipient also receives AFDC benefits (or benefits from other transfer programs), as earnings increase the family experiences a simultaneous reduction in both AFDC benefits and the food stamp bonus. However, since AFDC benefits are taken into account as income when figuring the food stamp purchase price, the reduction is less than if AFDC were not so counted.

In the past five years, the number of food stamp beneficiaries has increased from less than 2 million in 1968 to more than 13 million in 1973. The program has recently been mandated nationwide, which will significantly increase both the eligible and the participating population. Expenditures are estimated to rise to $5 billion in FY 75 and beyond in FY 76, with more than 20 million participating and more than 35 million eligible. Food stamps now play a major role in the transfer system. The program covers the working poor as well as the categorical welfare poor. This broad coverage, along with the desire on society's part to ensure that the benefit is used to buy food, makes alterations in the existing system difficult to design. The Administration's 1969 welfare reform proposal, the Family Assistance Plan (FAP), would have made some families worse off because the basic benefit plus state supplement combined with the cashed-out food stamps would have been less than current AFDC benefits plus the food stamp bonus in certain states.

MEDICAID

The basic legislative objective of Medicaid (or medical assistance) is to enable states, at their option, to furnish medical assistance to welfare recipients (needy families with dependent children and the aged, blind, and disabled) and the medically indigent (defined below). The program is administered by the states and jointly financed by the federal government and the states under a complex sharing formula. The federal appropriation for Medicaid is open-ended. Generally, benefits are in the form of payments to providers of medical care services, with the reimbursable services specified by the states. There is considerable variation in average benefits across demographic and categorical groups. Since states have considerable flexibility in setting elegibility limits and benefit coverage and since the cost and availability of medical care vary, there are wide variations among states, as is shown by the estimate for FY 72 in Table 3.

TABLE 3: AVERAGE MEDICAL VENDOR PAYMENTS PER FAMILY, FISCAL YEAR 1972

Average Medical Vendor Payment per Family	*Number of States**
Less than $100	1
$100 – 249	7
$250 – 399	5
$400 – 549	16
$550 – 699	5
$700 – 849	9
$850 – 999	6
$1000 and over	3

Source: *Charles L. Schultze et al.,* Setting National Priorities: The 1973 Budget *(Washington, D.C.: The Brookings Institution, 1973), p. 219.*

**Data include Washington, D.C., Guam, Puerto Rico, Virgin Islands, and Hawaii, and exclude Alaska and Arizona.*

Average medical payments for families eligible for AFDC are estimated to range from $50 per family in Mississippi to $1,150 per family in California. In February 1973, New York, California, and Michigan accounted for almost 42 percent of all Medicaid expenditures.

Public assistance recipients are automatically eligible for Medicaid. States can also secure federal support to cover families that do not receive money payments but are in eligible categories (AFDC, aged, blind, disabled) and whose income minus medical expenses is less than 133 percent of the needs standard in that state for cash assistance. Such eligible persons and families are called the medically indigent.

Public assistance recipients fully retain Medicaid benefits as long as public assistance eligibility is maintained. As soon as income exceeds the welfare breakeven, Medicaid status changes from full benefits to no benefits in states without a separate program for the medically indigent.[12] These eligibility rules for Medicaid result in a serious "notch" effect, whereby families can find themselves ineligible for benefits of considerable value simply by moving off of cash assistance or increasing their income slightly. This can create an extremely strong disincentive to increased work effort.[13]

There is general public acceptance of the fact that our present health-financing system is inadequate, particularly for the low-income population. Several proposals for a form of national health insurance, including one submitted by the Administration, are currently being considered in Congress.

HOUSING

Another primary component of the welfare system is housing. At present there are a variety of federal housing assistance programs ranging from supply efforts, such as public housing, to the more recent demand-oriented experimental allowances. The major income-conditioned housing assistance programs often are characterized by eligibility criteria and benefit structures that relate local housing costs to tenant income. Typically there is a rental charge that is set at 25 percent of income with a maximum at the "market rent" (or at cost for housing owned by the local government or a nonprofit organization). The difference between the rental charge and the market rent is the subsidy, which falls to zero when 25 percent of income equals the market rent. This net benefit reduction as income rises is structured in much the same way as in the food stamp program. The form and face value of the benefit remains constant while the price varies and acts as the welfare tax on income.

In FY 73, the combined budget for the various housing assistance programs is estimated to be about $2.0 billion and is tied to specific housing units—about 2.2 million of them. In recent years, these housing programs have come under increased criticism. First, they are inequitable. There are substantially fewer subsidized housing units than there are families eligible to occupy them: less than 10 percent of these households eligible for housing assistance receive it. Second, these housing programs give the consumer little or no choice among housing alternatives since the programs provide indirect subsidies that are funneled through the suppliers of housing services to the recipients. The recognition of these and other shortcomings has led the Department of Housing and Urban Development to experiment with various types of housing allowances that provide direct assistance to low-income households. A housing task force has been reexamining the various rationales for a government role in the housing market, reviewing the objectives and performance of existing programs, and considering alternative strategies for attaining housing goals. It seems likely that the notion of direct cash assistance for housing may play a major role in future housing policy debates and should be considered, along with current housing programs, in welfare reform discussions.[14]

SUPPLEMENTAL SECURITY INCOME (SSI)

The SSI program, which went into effect January 1, 1974, replaced the existing categorical programs (state-administered with federal financial participation) providing assistance to the aged, blind, and disabled. It represents a major departure from the existing system in that the federal government is assuming primary responsibility for financial assistance to that population, and is also administering the program.

The key provisions of the program are a nationally uniform federal benefit level, a 50 percent benefit reduction rate, nationally uniform eligibility requirements, incentives for state supplementation of the basic benefit level, federal administration of the basic benefit together with incentives for federal administration of state supplements, and fiscal relief for the states.

SSI thus approaches a national federally administered program. It will, however, fall somewhat short since, because of state supplementation, there will still be interstate differences in benefit levels not necessarily related to cost of living differences. In addition, because some states have opted to administer their supplement, there will be duplicative administrative structures.

The SSI program also interacts with AFDC. The dependents of SSI recipients cannot be covered under SSI, but may be covered by AFDC. Disabled children under 18 years of age, some of whom are in AFDC families, are now eligible for SSI benefits (they were eligible under the old Aid to the Disabled program). Thus some families will receive benefits from both SSI and AFDC.

The strengths and weaknesses of the SSI administrative model will provide experience directly relevant to an evaluation of the administrative alternatives for other cash assistance programs.

OTHER PROGRAMS

In addition to the five programs described above, there are numerous other income-tested federally financed programs that provide benefits to the poor. These programs generally provide benefits in the form of goods or services rather than cash. Included in this group are the food distribution program, child nutrition, health programs that provide direct services, child care services—provided by Head Start, the Work Incentive Programs (WIN), and as a social service to cash assistance recipients—legal services, various social services, and manpower training services—WIN, the Manpower Development and Training Act (MDTA), Concentrated Employment Program (CEP), Neighborhood Youth Corps (NYC), and Job Opportunities in the Business Sector (JOBS), for example. Eligibility for some of these services is closely tied to eligibility for the cash assistance programs—WIN, social services, and some day care programs are examples. Since many of these programs are administered by other agencies independent of the cash assistance programs, there are often no controls on overlapping coverage. Some families participate in many programs, while others participate in one or two or none at all. A welfare reform effort must consider how all these programs should be integrated into a new structure.

Finally, most states and localities finance cash transfers under a variety of programs referred to as General Assistance.[15] Frequently, General Assistance is limited to short-term or emergency assistance, but in some states—New York, for example—continuing aid is provided to the working poor. General Assistance permits local jurisdictions to attempt to meet local needs. It is one program that must be taken into account when the federal government considers redesigning or replacing the welfare system.

The Incidence of Poverty and the Coverage of the Transfer System by Family Type

Data collected recently by the University of Michigan Survey Research Center allows us to compare the incidence of poverty among family types and to evaluate the adequacy of the transfer system in alleviating poverty.[16]

Table 4 shows the number and percentage of families[17] whose incomes before transfers were below the poverty standard in 1971. Clearly, families with a non-aged, nondisabled male head were the least likely of all to have private incomes below the

TABLE 4: NUMBER AND PERCENTAGE FAMILIES WITH INCOMES BELOW POVERTY LEVEL BEFORE TRANSFERS, AND NUMBER AND PERCENTAGE RECEIVING TRANSFERS, 1971

	Total Families in U.S.	*Families with Incomes Below Poverty Standard Before Transfers**	*Percentage Families Below Poverty Standard Before Transfers**	*Pretransfer Poor Families Receiving Transfers*	*Percentage Pretransfer Poor Families Receiving Transfers*	*Percentage Pretransfer Poor Families Not Receiving Transfers*
	(thousands)	(thousands)		(thousands)		
All families	72,046	15,059	21	12,095	80	20
Families with aged head	12,974	6,977	54	6,773	97	3
Families with non-aged, disabled head	3,567	2,041	57	1,823	89	11
Families with non-aged, nondisabled head without children	24,129	2,356	10	1,009	43	57
Families with non-aged, nondisabled male head with children	26,671	1,659	6	815	49	51
Families with non-aged, nondisabled female head with children	4,706	2,027	43	1,676	83	17

Notes: *Families include childless couples and unrelated individuals.*
Transfers are benefits from both social insurance and welfare programs, including state General Assistance.
**This contrasts with our more usual measurements of poverty which show the percentage of families whose incomes including transfers are below the poverty standard.*

TABLE 5: EXTENT OF POVERTY ALLEVIATION BY SOCIAL INSURANCE PROGRAMS

	Families with Pretransfer Income Below Poverty Standard	*Pretransfer Poor Families Made Nonpoor by Social Insurance Benefits*	*Percentage Pretransfer Poor Families Made Nonpoor by Social Insurance Benefits*	*Families Remaining Poor After Social Insurance Benefits*	*Percentage Pretransfer Poor Families Remaining Poor After Social Insurance Benefits*
	(thousands)	(thousands)		(thousands)	
All families	15,059	4,770	32	10,290	68
Families with aged head	6,977	3,629	52	3,348	48*
Families with non-aged, disabled head	2,041	401	20	1,640	80*
Families with non-aged, nondisabled head without children	2,356	416	18	1,940	82
Families with non-aged, nondisabled male head with children	1,659	107	6	1,552	94
Families with non-aged, nondisabled female head with children	2,027	216	11	1,811	89

Notes: *Families include childless couples and unrelated individuals.*
Transfers are benefits from social insurance and welfare programs.
**Pattern will shift due to SSI program.*

poverty standard while those with heads who were aged, disabled and/or female were the most likely to be in poverty.[18]

What percentage of these pretransfer poor families receive any transfers at all? The answer to this question is important because the higher the percentage that receive some transfers, the more one would look to increasing benefits of existing programs to increase the adequacy of coverage. On the other hand, the lower the percentage, the more one might look to broadening categorical eligibility criteria so more poor would be included. Table 4 shows the percentage of pretransfer poor families in each category who receive some transfers. As might be expected, given the categorical nature of our current transfer system, some poor families are much more likely to receive transfer benefits than others. Coverage is best for the poor aged, disabled, and female-headed families with children; only 3 percent, 11 percent, and 17 percent, respectively, received no transfer payments. In contrast, 51 percent of poor male-headed families with children and 57 percent of poor families with a non-aged, nondisabled head without children received no transfer benefits.

Within the category of those receiving some transfers, there is considerable variation in the number of programs from which families are receiving benefits. For example, a recent survey by the General Accounting Office (GAO) of selected low-income areas[19] (which probably have greater program coverage than other areas) found between 60 percent and 75 percent of recipient households benefited from more than one program and between 10 percent and 25 percent received benefits from five or more programs.[20]

How adequate are the transfers (both social insurance and welfare benefits) received by these families? While several measures of adequacy might be used, these tables show the percentage of each family type whose total incomes were raised above the poverty threshold through the receipt of transfer benefits. Table 5 shows the extent of poverty alleviation by the social insurance programs (principally Social Security and unemployment compensation). Not surprisingly, these programs were most effective in the case of the aged. Table 6 allows us to look at the antipoverty effectiveness of welfare benefits (the cash and food stamp programs) as distinguished from the social insurance programs. It shows the percentage of pretransfer poor families raised out of poverty by social insurance and welfare programs combined. The percentage of poverty alleviation for the total population of pretransfer poor is 32 percent for social insurance programs alone,

TABLE 6: ANTIPOVERTY EFFECTIVENESS OF WELFARE BENEFITS (CASH PROGRAMS AND FOOD STAMPS) AND SOCIAL INSURANCE PROGRAMS COMBINED

	Families with Pretransfer Income Below Poverty Standard	*Pretransfer Poor Families Made Nonpoor by Receipt of Transfers*	*Percentage Pretransfer Poor Families Made Nonpoor by Receipt of Transfers*	*Families Remaining Poor After Transfers*	*Percentage Pretransfer Poor Families Remaining Poor After Transfers*
	(thousands)	*(thousands)*		*(thousands)*	
All families	15,059	6,432	43	8,627	57
Families with aged head	6,977	4,006	57	2,971	43*
Families with non-aged, disabled head	2,041	745	36	1,296	64*
Families with non-aged, nondisabled head without children	2,356	536	23	1,820	77
Families with non-aged, nondisabled male head with children	1,659	355	21	1,304	79
Families with non-aged, nondisabled female head with children	2,027	790	39	1,237	61

Notes: *Families include childless couples and unrelated individuals.*
Transfers are benefits from both social insurance and welfare programs.
**Pattern will shift due to SSI program.*

and is increased only to 43 percent with welfare programs included. The receipt of welfare benefits removes from poverty only 16 percent of the families who would have been poor in the absence of the welfare system. Looking at specific family types, adding in the benefits from the welfare system has very little impact on decreasing the percentage of aged and childless families in poverty. It has the greatest impact on female-headed families with children. The transfer system as a whole raises 39 percent of the pretransfer poor female-headed families with children above the poverty standard. It should be emphasized that these data are not intended to be all-inclusive: benefits from other programs, such as subsidized housing and Medicaid, are not included. Furthermore, the data may not be precisely accurate: Recipients may be underreporting their transfer incomes.

TABLE 7: TYPES OF FAMILIES REMAINING POOR AFTER TRANSFERS

	Total Families in U.S.	*Families Remaining Poor After Transfers*	*Percentage Families Remaining Poor After Transfers*
	(thousands)	(thousands)	
All families	72,046	8,627	12
Families with aged head	12,974	2,971	23*
Families with non-aged, disabled head	3,567	1,296	36*
Families with non-aged, nondisabled head without children	24,129	1,820	8
Families with non-aged, nondisabled male head with children	26,671	1,304	5
Families with non-aged, nondisabled female head with children	4,706	1,237	26

Notes: *Families include childless couples and unrelated individuals.*
Transfers are benefits received from both social insurance and welfare programs.
**Pattern will shift due to SSI program.*

In summary, Table 6 shows that the transfer system does not remove all recipient families from poverty. In fact, while 80 percent of all pretransfer poor families received some transfer benefits, only 43 percent were raised above the poverty standard by these transfers. Fifty-seven percent of pretransfer poor families remain poor either because they did not receive transfers at all or because the level of transfers was not sufficient to raise their income above the poverty standard.

Table 7 gives us the breakdown by family type of those families that remain in poverty even after transfers. The percentage of poverty incidence is highest for families with aged or disabled heads[21] and female-headed families with children. The distribution of individuals living in poor families differs from that of the families themselves, as family sizes vary by family type.

TABLE 8: AVERAGE FAMILY SIZE AND NUMBER OF INDIVIDUALS IN FAMILIES REMAINING POOR AFTER TRANSFERS

	Families Remaining Poor After Transfers	*Average Number of Individuals in Family*	*Individuals Living in Poor Families**
	(thousands)		(thousands)
All families	8,627	2.77	23,900
Families with aged head	2,971	1.72	5,100
Families with non-aged, disabled head	1,296	3.06	4,000
Families with non-aged, nondisabled male head without children	1,820	1.31	2,400
Families with non-aged, nondisabled male head with children	1,304	5.48	7,100
Families with non-aged, nondisabled female head with children	1,237	4.30	5,300

Notes: *Families include childless couples and unrelated individuals.*
Transfers are benefits received from both social insurance and welfare programs.
**Rounded to nearest hundred.*

Table 8 shows the average family size and the number of individuals living in poor families. More than one-half of all individuals living in poor families live in families with children in which the family head is neither aged nor disabled; the majority of these families have both parents present.

In sum, the data reveal that the coverage and benefit levels of the current transfer system are considerably less than adequate in terms of raising poor families above poverty thresholds. The social insurance programs, although not targeted for this purpose, have had considerably more impact than the welfare programs in reducing poverty. Furthermore, the coverage of the current transfer system is very uneven; childless couples with a non-aged, nondisabled head and families with children headed by a non-aged, nondisabled male are the least likely to receive benefits.

Characteristics of the Welfare System

The previous sections have described the major components of the welfare system, the coverage of those individual component programs, and the extent of multiple program participation. In this section the discussion focuses on a summation of the characteristics of the system that may be inconsistent with overall principles of equity and efficiency.

GEOGRAPHIC DIFFERENCES

Interstate and intrastate differences in eligibility, benefit levels, and administration are perhaps the inevitable (and not necessarily undesirable) result of the decentralized federal-state structure that characterizes much of the current welfare system. As indicated earlier, the practical effect of this structure is that similar families in similar circumstances can receive very different treatment depending solely on their place of residence. Differences are primarily based on the relative desires and capabilities of political subdivisions to assist their needy populations and only partially on cost of living differentials. Many observers have been concerned that this large variance in benefit levels has affected the migration patterns of the poor, although there is little conclusive evidence to that effect.

The variation in average monthly AFDC benefits per recipient has been noted, from $82.71 in New York to $14.40 in Mississippi in April 1973. Under the Medicaid program, estimated average yearly medical payments per family ranged from $1,150 in California to $50 in Mississippi. In the past there has been some variation in the eligibility requirements and income definitions for the food stamp program; however, in 1971 eligibility requirements, income definitions, and the benefit structure were made uniform throughout the country. Under the public housing program the local authorities have the sole authority for defining income for the purposes of eligibility and rental charges, and thus the net benefit structure; housing benefits are, however, systematically related to local housing costs.

The desirability of eliminating interstate differences depends in part on attitudes toward decentralization and federal-state relationships, in part on concerns for equity among recipients, and in part on the degree of interest in ensuring that any additional federal dollars are targeted on the most needy of recipients. (Should the federal government be spending transfer dollars on families with incomes at the $10,000 level in New York while not doing so for those at the $2,000 level in Mississippi?) It seems that a decision must be made among options that range from complete decentralization (as in General Assistance), to partial decentralization (AFDC), to federal standards (food stamps), and to complete federalization (SSI) with state supplementation possible.

THE IMPACT OF CATEGORIZATION

The purpose of categorization is target efficiency, that is, to assure that the benefits of a program are received, to the extent possible, by that group presumed to be in need. The exclusion of certain groups is thus a natural consequence of this approach. Categorization can be useful to the extent that a target group can be separated from the rest of the population; at the same time incentives for undesirable "self-selection" into the target group should be prevented. The latter is one of the serious problems that can accompany categorization.

SSI can be relatively effective in categorization because the target group is defined by relatively objective criteria (age, blindness, disability) that are directly related to a person's ability to earn. Furthermore, it is unlikely that many persons would or could change their characteristics to become eligible for SSI.

On the other hand, the AFDC categorization process is less effective. As explained earlier, AFDC benefits are provided only to a certain category of poor persons: families in which there is a dependent child who has been deprived of parental support. Single persons and childless couples are not eligible. Intact families with heads who work more than 100 hours a month at low wages—the working poor—are also not eligible for benefits. In 27 states, welfare benefits are not provided to intact families with unemployed heads. In the 23 states with the AFDC-UF program, benefits are not provided to an unemployed father if he is eligible for unemployment compensation. These eligibility criteria are not directly related to ability to earn, and because they are more easily manipulated, incentives are created for people to alter their behavior in order to qualify for benefits. The head of an intact family, for example, can increase his family's income by leaving home, thus making the family eligible for benefits. There is very little evidence, however, on the extent to which the categorical nature of AFDC actually leads to family breakup or fewer family formations. It is also not clear what effect more vigorous attempts to obtain child support from absent fathers would have on preventing family breakup. California has recently instituted several measures aimed at this problem. The cost-effectiveness of this approach should be evaluated.

Categorization can also result in gaps and overlaps in coverage. In the current system there is no cash assistance available to the working poor family with a head who works full time, though the income of this family may be less than the income of an AFDC family with a nonworking head. Other instances of uneven coverage were demonstrated earlier in the paper.

In discussing the coverage of the system, one must also take into account the in-kind benefits provided by programs that were not included in the SRC data cited.[22] Among these are subsidized housing, Medicaid, manpower services, and social services. Data on the coverage of these programs are not readily available. Furthermore, it is not clear whether it is always appropriate to regard the per capita expenditures (that is, government cost) for in-kind transfers such as manpower services as income to the participant.

The General Accounting Office survey of multiple program participation conducted for the JEC[23] showed that when families participated in numerous programs (five or more), their total benefits were relatively high. However, such participation was most uneven, and the distribution of benefits was not directly related to need, with many families receiving far less than needed and others more.

Another problem sometimes results from differences between eligibility for admission to a program and eligibility for continued participation. For example, assuming the presence of a dependent child and assets below the allowable limit, eligibility for AFDC is determined by comparing current income to the needs standard. If a female family head is employed and earning more than the needs standard, her family is ineligible for benefits. She may, however, be working alongside a woman with the same earned income and family size who receives AFDC benefits because she was on AFDC *before* starting work. The income disregards and work-related expense deductions then enable her to earn income well beyond the needs standards. Such results may provide the person without eligibility with strong incentives to leave work (at least temporarily) in order to achieve eligibility.

DISINCENTIVES

Work disincentives have been a major concern of the welfare reform effort. Few would argue with the notion that the welfare system should be designed to encourage those who can work to do so. While there is an argument as to the proper mix of market incentives and work requirements, it seems reasonable to expect that a welfare recipient who works should increase his disposable income as a result of his efforts. In fact, the system has certain features that actively discourage work. These take two forms: "notches" and high cumulative benefit reduction rates. A notch, as noted earlier, occurs when a small change in income results in a precipitous change in benefits. Two examples of severe notches in the welfare system relating to the AFDC-UF and Medicaid programs, were already described.

The father receiving AFDC-UF benefits might well think twice about a part-time job that would provide 105 hours of work a month at the minimum wage. Accepting the job would make him ineligible for AFDC-UF benefits. The recipient about to lose all Medicaid benefits because of a modest salary increase might consider how to avoid being made worse off because she was about to earn more.

Notches do, however, have a rationale. First, they can limit costs by limiting coverage. Second, within these cost constraints they can enable *full* benefits to be provided to everyone on welfare; as in the case of Medicaid, there is no benefit decline as income rises. Third, they can avoid the extension of benefits to certain persons above the poverty level. Against these arguments must be weighed the negative impact of the notches on work incentives, promoting a response to the system that is directly counter to its objectives. The equity of providing extensive benefits to some persons and none to others who are at substantially the same income level, should also be considered.

Linking benefits more closely to income, an approach now in use in some programs, provides a partial solution to this problem. Program benefits, rather than being "on-off," decline gradually as income rises. This type of benefit structure is a part of most of the major programs—AFDC, food stamps, public housing—and is a major feature of the Administration's new health insurance proposal. However, this solution only partially alleviates the work disincentive problem, since a family that participates in several programs also faces several benefit reductions as a result of an increase in earnings. A reduction in AFDC benefits, increases in food stamp purchase price and the public housing rent, along with other net benefit reductions can take a very large bite out of increased earnings, and can, in fact, have the net effect of reducing disposable income. Consider an intact family of four in New York City that participates in the cash assistance program (AFDC-UF and New York City Home Relief, in this example), food stamps, school lunch, Medicaid, and public housing.[24] The family head works part time and earns $3,000. If he earns an extra $1,000, family disposable income will be *reduced* by $231. If he *reduces* his earnings by $1,000, the net loss of disposable income will be only $60. Over the range of earnings from zero to $5,000, a $1,000 increase in earnings will increase disposable income by *at most* $91. The cumulative benefit reduction rate in this example is an extremely high one.[25] However, such a high rate does not apply to the overwhelming majority of families currently receiving transfer payments. But it does apply to some. Moreover, if programs continue to expand and proliferate as they have in the past, the example will apply to many more families.

BENEFITS IN CASH OR IN-KIND?

Inefficiencies due to the form of the transfer benefits (relative to the need presumably being met) are undoubtedly prevalent in the welfare system. However, measuring precisely the degree of inefficiency is difficult. Would it be more cost-effective to provide vouchers to welfare recipients who request them for child care and let the market operate, or to provide the care directly through the public sector?[26] The existence of a multiplicity of programs each providing a different type of transfer to overlapping target populations is probably not the result of a process in which the needs of these populations as a whole were considered and in which the most efficient set of transfer forms and related programs was structured to meet these needs. The existence of different programs with different transfer forms may be explained in part by several factors: by the historical timing of both the manifestation of a particular concern of society and the existence of sufficient resources to meet the concern; by the desire to restrict recipients' use of public transfer dollars to particular purposes; by the lobbying strengths of various interest groups; and by the vagaries of the agency structure of the executive branch and the committee structure of Congress. In any event, whatever the reasons and rationales for their existence, the present multiplicity of transfer forms must be considered undesirable when viewed from the various perspectives involved.

ADMINISTRATIVE EFFICIENCY

Another characteristic of the present welfare system is administrative overlap and inefficiencies among programs comprising the system. These problems can be viewed partly as a consequence of the categorical strategy and the multiplicity of transfer benefits provided, but they result as well from the independence, subjectivity, and lack of coordination among the various programs.

The relationship between effective categorization and objective eligibility criteria becomes more apparent when social insurance and welfare programs are compared. The eligibility criteria for Social Security are straightforward, and to a large extent, they involve historical rather than current data: age, contributions, and quarters of participation. In some instances, benefits are adjusted to current earnings, but these earnings are important for only a relatively small percentage of recipients. Because program administration can be based primarily on unambiguous standards and historical information, administration is simplified enormously.

A program like AFDC differs from Social Security in requiring current, rather than historical, information and in having standards that may be unambiguous in theory but that are hard to verify in practice. Consider again the following examples:

- If a single-parent family is to be eligible for AFDC, the family income and family assets must be below cutoff levels and the father in the family must be dead, incapacitated, or continuously absent from home. Certain elements of income and assets are easily checked, but some—like casual income paid in cash or a car temporarily registered to somebody else—are unverifiable. Proving that a man is not continuously absent from the home is equally difficult.

- If a two-parent family is to be eligible for AFDC, the father must be incapacitated or, in the 23 states with AFDC-UF, working less than 100 hours per month. He must not have refused a bona fide job offer that would have allowed him to work more hours. Is the father actually incapacitated? How many hours is a man really working? How many bona fide job offers has he received? If the man does not give accurate answers, information will be hard to come by.

Both of these examples highlight the problems encountered when the eligibility criteria require a subjective determination and depend on characteristics that are subject to frequent changes. This complexity leads to complicated procedures. One of the JEC studies notes, for example, that processing a welfare applicant in Atlanta requires filling out as many as 27 different forms.[27]

Alternatively, a system that relaxes categorization and relies more on income levels for eligibility could reduce administrative costs. If a father does not have to be absent from the home for the family to qualify for benefits, then there is no administrative need to check on the father's presence. While administrative cost would be reduced, the program coverage and cost would be consequently increased. Trade-offs like these are inherent in any transfer program.

Our current system of multiple, loosely coordinated programs compounds administrative effort. The AFDC program uses one set of eligibility criteria and income definitions,[28] the food stamp program uses a second set, and public housing a third. This inefficiency may be acceptable if for some reason it is necessary. However, eligibility criteria and income definitions do not always differ among programs for rational reasons. Differences emerge primarily because the programs were created and structured independently without much regard for the administrative efficiency that could be realized through common eligibility criteria and common program definitions, where feasible and desirable.

Further, common information gathering could be established even where differential application is necessary.

When combined with the complex and subjective criteria for eligibility and benefit determination that exist in individual programs, uncoordinated and duplicative administration increases the likelihood of undetected error and fraud—although fraud, as legally defined, does not appear to be substantial. Errors in eligibility determination and benefit calculations are more serious, and work to increase and reduce benefits. The Department of Health, Education, and Welfare has launched a major effort to reduce errors in AFDC by streamlining procedures and instituting the Quality Control Sampling System.[29] While this will reduce the errors resulting from the internal complexities of AFDC, it will have less impact on errors that result from uncoordinated and duplicative administration of overlapping programs. Those problems are best addressed by better program integration. The techniques available to accomplish that objective are described in Chapter 7.

TARGET INEFFICIENCIES

As previous discussion and data have indicated, the monies expended through the welfare system, while providing very substantial income supplementation to the poor, are not very target efficient. The effect of geographical variations, categorization, and multiple program participation were elaborated on above. In addition, some of the programs, particularly food stamps and AFDC, contain very liberal disregards for certain types of income that can result in a family of four retaining eligibility at income levels in excess of $10,000 per year.

Finally, target inefficiencies have been introduced into the transfer system as a whole (social insurance and welfare) as a result of the utilization of the social insurance system as a vehicle to accomplish welfare objectives. This has occurred largely because of the inadequacies of our welfare system. The existence of higher minimum benefit levels and the loosening of eligibility criteria in both the UI and OASDI systems beyond those easily justifiable as social insurance objectives were partially a result of the lack of adequate coverage by the welfare system of the aged and intact family heads and a result of the desire to remove as large a proportion of the aged as possible from the need to undergo a means test. However, because the social insurance programs are not income-tested to any great extent, they are inefficient vehicles for achieving welfare objectives. Most increases in such programs, even if used to increase minimum benefit levels or extend eligibility to groups with less previous attachment to the labor force, will go to families well above the poverty level. Equivalent increased benefits in welfare programs would be highly targeted on needy families or individuals.

Providing smaller benefits to the near poor than to the poor is not necessarily target inefficient if the goal is a more equal distribution of income (as opposed to the alleviation of poverty) or replacement of interrupted earnings. In the case of UI and Social Security, however, the benefits are going to only some of the near poor, and these benefits are often larger than the benefits that go to the poor. In fact, some of the poor continue to receive no transfers at all.

As was indicated in the earlier discussion of social insurance, a considerable strengthening of the ability of this system to perform its primary objective—earnings replacement—is in order. However, proposals that extend these programs in an attempt to aid the low-income population should be approached cautiously. While factors such as political acceptability have to be considered, target efficiency should be more carefully weighed than it has been in the past.

GENERAL

Due to the multiplicity of programs comprising the welfare system, many with overlapping target populations, its overall effects are difficult to understand and, in many cases, are not those intended by the designers of some of its components. Furthermore, many different Congressional committees have oversight of its various components, and few of them need concern themselves explicitly with the overall resource constraints of the total system. Thus, it is virtually impossible to promulgate a coherent strategy for the whole system, one that reflects a considered compromise among the somewhat conflicting objectives and the limited resources available to achieve them.

Goals of an Income-Tested Welfare System

In the preceding section, several problems caused by structural features of individual programs and interactions among programs were discussed. Perceptions of exactly what problem areas constitute the "welfare mess" and how welfare reform should proceed depend largely on the goals established for an income-tested transfer system. Although there is likely to be disagreement about relative priorities and the means of accomplishment, hopefully there can be fairly general agreement about the desirability of several general principles. The following is a list of criteria, admittedly incomplete, that includes those most frequently mentioned in welfare reform debates:

ADEQUACY

An income-tested transfer system should be designed in tandem with the employment and social insurance systems so that people who can work and people who cannot work have access to a level of income that provides some minimum level of adequacy. (Unfortunately, adequacy is not only hard to agree upon, it is hard to measure.) The design of the system has to reflect a realistic assessment of what our employment and social and private insurance systems are accomplishing—and can be expected to accomplish.

TARGET EFFICIENCY

Benefits should be accurately targeted on those most in need. Within a given budget constraint, greater benefits should be transferred to those with lower incomes. Trade-offs between possible increases in certain kinds of expenditures on social insurance programs (those directed specifically at low-income groups) or income-tested transfer programs should be carefully considered in this regard.

ADMINISTRATIVE EFFICIENCY

The system should obtain its objectives at a minimum cost. It should be straightforward to administer, combining administrative functions into a single unit, when possible. If multiple programs are required, then a high degree of coordination and integration should exist among programs serving the same populations. These measures would control administrative costs and make the system more manageable and accessible. It is important to note that simplicity for the recipient is as desirable as for the administrators; both should be implemented, if possible.

HORIZONTAL EQUITY

People in similar circumstances should be treated similarly. Categorization is one way of defining similar circumstances; yet as has been seen, administrative discretion and program rules can cause inequities. Wide interstate benefit differentials might also be considered inequitable. In addition, gaps in categorical coverage, which have left some families and individuals ineligible for assistance while others with generally similar characteristics are eligible for benefits, should be remedied. Such horizontal inequities and ineffective categorization can create incentives for undesirable behavior, such as family splitting. The total income of families with the head working full time should be greater than that of families not putting out any work effort but who are receiving income-tested transfer income.

VERTICAL EQUITY

Persons and families who earn more should receive more total income than those earning less. Those with relatively greater needs should receive relatively greater assistance. This principle of vertical equity must be carefully integrated with the following principle.

WORK INCENTIVES

People who are able to work should find it strongly in their interest to do so. The system should encourage self-sufficiency. Thus, those who work and earn more should have substantially higher disposable incomes. Recipients who work should not be penalized for working as has been the case due to notches and high cumulative benefit reduction rates in the present welfare system. On the other hand, the basic benefit level of an income supplementation plan for those already working may be a partial disincentive to work (at least for secondary workers), even if marginal benefit reduction rates are kept low.[30]

FAMILY STABILITY INCENTIVES

Any new system should minimize disincentives to family formation and eliminate possible incentives for family breakup. As noted, one of the serious problems that can accompany a categorical program is that people may be encouraged to "self-select" themselves into the target group.

INDEPENDENCE

Promotion of independence for the recipient, while often considered a most important goal of an income-tested transfer system, is difficult to translate into operational terms. However, the system ought to be structured in such a way that it aids and encourages individuals and families who are able to become self-sufficient, so they will no longer require assistance.

COHERENCY AND CONTROL

The system as a whole should be understandable in its operation and effect, should have the effect intended, and should be subject to policy and fiscal control.

CONCLUSION

These goals should serve as the basis for evaluating the structuring or restructuring of a welfare system. It must be emphasized, however, that these goals are not fully consistent with each other. For example, enhancing work incentives by eliminating notches and lowering cumulative benefit reduction rates, without reducing benefit levels, means that breakeven incomes are raised. More benefits then go to persons in relatively higher income classes, thereby decreasing target efficiency. If instead, benefit levels are lowered, the adequacy of the system is reduced. Trade-offs such as these are unfortunate but unavoidable. The need for this welfare reform effort is to a great extent a direct result of failure to foresee the consequences of conflicting goals and political pressures and to face the realities of interrelated program decisions.

Supplement: The Dynamics of the Low-Income Population

This supplement presents some data on (1) the extent to which families[31] move in and out of poverty and (2) the extent to which families move on and off the AFDC rolls, and indicates some reasons for these shifts. More complete data than has been available heretofore indicate a high degree of income fluctuation in the low-income population. Some of the implications of these results are discussed briefly following the summary of the major findings.

INCOME STABILITY

The information on the income stability of the poverty population was compiled by the Panel Study in Income Dynamics recently completed by the University of Michigan Survey Research

Center (SRC) for the Office of Economic Opportunity.[32] That study analyzed data from five annual surveys, which included information on various economic, demographic, and other variables for a group of 5,000 households (including unrelated individuals) that were selected to be representative of the entire United States population for the period 1967-1971. Over this period the incidence of poverty in the sample declined from 12.7 percent to 10.6 percent, which is quite close to the degree of decline reported in national figures compiled by the Bureau of the Census.

According to the SRC study, about 32 percent of those households who were poor in 1967 remained poor for the four following years, 14 percent escaped poverty by a wide margin (steady growth in income over the period to more than 1.5 times the relevant poverty threshold), 12 percent experienced steady growth in income but ended the period between the poverty threshold and 1.5 times their poverty threshold, and 42 percent were nonpoor for at least one year but with no consistent pattern.

Since there was a very small decline in the percentage who were poor over this period, the number of individuals entering poverty in any one year was approximately equal to the number that were leaving poverty. Over this period, 17 percent of the household population were "at risk," which means that they had incomes below the poverty level in at least one of the five years and averaged less than 1.5 times their poverty threshold for the entire period.[33] This is in contrast to the 10.6 percent to 12.7 percent figure for the number of families in poverty at any given time during this five-year period. Another 3 percent were never poor, but averaged less than 1.5 times the poverty standard, and so might also be considered "at risk" with regard to poverty.

How does this incidence vary by family type? Using the broader definition of being "at risk" discussed above, 43 percent of persons in aged families and 47 percent of persons in female-headed families with children, but only 13 percent of persons in male-headed families were "at risk" over this period.

Which family types had the most unstable income patterns? In general, of those who were poor in 1967, persons living in aged families were most likely to remain poor over the five-year period. Those living in female-headed families were more likely to fluctuate in and out of poverty, and those living in male-headed families were the most likely to so fluctuate.

What were the major causes of this income instability? In the case of persons living in male-headed families in 1967 who suffered a decline in income over the five-year period and ended in poverty, more than 80 percent of the cases can be explained by a change in family composition, the incurring of a disability, or the passing of age 65. Persons in male-headed families as of 1967 who moved out of poverty over this period were primarily either those in families with a young head in an upward phase of his lifetime earnings cycle or those who moved out of poor households and formed new families with fewer members and perhaps greater earning power.

In the case of persons living in female-headed families as of 1967, an important reason for downward movement seems to be disablement (which in these data includes pregnancy). More than half of the upward movement out of poverty for such individuals was due to their living in a family that acquired a male head during the five-year period.

Data about and reasons for the income instability of the poverty population are summarized below.

- One's risk of being in poverty is highly related to the type of family in which one lives.

- There are large year-to-year fluctuations in income in the low-income population. Less than one-third of those families initially poor in the survey sample remained poor over the five-year period.

- A large amount of this income instability is due to changes in demographic characteristics of the family, especially the age and health status of the head and the number of parents present. For example, fluctuations in income are greatest for those living in non-aged, male-headed families and smallest for those living in aged families.

A few tentative policy implications for poverty programs can be advanced on the basis of these limited data.

- Any programs restricted to those in poverty (or, indeed, below any low-income line) are likely to have an eligible population that is highly variable, since incomes fluctuate widely. The variability of the eligible population will be even greater if eligibility is also categorically determined by demographic characteristics (the aged excepted). This suggests that the administrative system of a poverty program should be designed to take into account the fact of frequent change.

- In general, the factors that cause families to exit from poverty are not amenable to direct manipulation by welfare programs (with the obvious exception of cash transfers).

- However, since demographic changes in families are such a powerful correlate with poverty risk, we should pay close attention to the indirect incentives that are built into the welfare system with regard to such changes.

VARIABILITY IN PROGRAM CLIENTELE

As just stated, the income instability of the poverty population implies variability in the clientele of any program with an income ceiling. An example of this can be found in the turnover of the AFDC caseload. There is no longitudinal survey for welfare recipients of the completeness of the Panel Study on Income Dynamics. Nonetheless, recent work begins to produce a picture of the dynamics of the welfare rolls.

The 1971 National Center for Social Statistics' AFDC sample produced a picture of the average participant family.[34] The average case had been opened about 1.5 years; 18 percent of the mothers either worked or were in training programs; the probability of the average family's leaving the welfare rolls within one year was 20 percent; and, once a family left the program, the chance of its returning at some future time was approximately 33 percent.

The probability of any one AFDC family leaving the rolls within the next year is related to a variety of family characteristics. In general, having more children and being nonwhite somewhat decrease the probability of a family's leaving the rolls within the next 12 months. However, the most important determinant is the length of time the family has already been on the rolls. The longer a family has been on the rolls, the lower the probability of leaving. For some categories, the probability declines dramatically with length of enrollment. Thus, for some families, AFDC does become a permanent way of life, but for most it appears to be a temporary backstop during a difficult period.

Like movement in and out of poverty, movement off the welfare rolls is often the result of large and discontinuous income changes, often resulting from factors unrelated to employment of the female head. Table 9 presents reasons for case discontinuance. It would appear that few mothers gradually work their way off the rolls. If they leave the rolls, it is, to a large degree, either because they have gone from not working to working full time, or because of changes in their income, need, or family status unrelated to the mother's employment. These results may not be surprising in view of the low wage that most welfare mothers can command and the high benefit reduction rates that provide little incentive for marginal increases in work effort.

These results indicate that many families leave welfare under the current system. The reasons they leave have a number of possible implications. The large importance of demographic changes (particularly in family composition) suggest that we should be careful to analyze the incentives (or disincentives) for such changes that exist in any current or proposed program and their effect. It also suggests that programs based on demographic categories cannot be expected to have an unchanging clientele.

In any event, it is apparent that there is considerable instability in both the welfare and the poverty populations. These are important facts to remember both in evaluating present programs and in designing new ones.

TABLE 9: REASONS FOR DISCONTINUING ASSISTANCE OF FEMALE-HEADED AFDC CASES

	Percentage
Employment of female head	11
Other changes in income	20
Changes in need	5
Changes in eligibility	30
Refusal to comply	10
Transfer to other program	4
Other	21
	100*

** Total exceeds 100 percent due to rounding.*

2

Programmatic Considerations and Options

The Form of Transfer Benefits

The current welfare system transfers benefits in several different forms: cash (SSI, AFDC), vouchers (food stamps), and goods and services (public housing, social services). It is by no means clear that in all cases the particular form of the transfer, chosen to meet particular consumption needs, is the most efficient for its purposes. In addition, many of the undesirable attributes of the welfare system arise because of the existence of a multitude of different means-tested (income-tested) transfer programs, with separate administrative structures, income definitions, and other characteristics, each program delivering a different type of benefit to different but highly overlapping target populations. The conditions under which various forms of transfers might be preferable to those in use are explored in order to provide a partial basis for a discussion of reshaping and simplifying the present welfare system with its plethora of component parts.

The point of departure for this discussion is an assertion that most of the unmet consumption needs of the low-income population arise simply from a lack of command over goods and services readily available in the market place but unaffordable for those with incomes below some minimum level of adequacy. Among these are clothing, transportation, food, many social services, and shelter.[35] This being the case, cash transfers to this population are the most efficient means to meet these particular needs for several reasons:

- Cash transfers minimize interference with the recipient's life and allow him to use the transfer to provide for those needs that he judges most acute.

- Cash transfers involve low administrative costs, compared with other types of transfers. Cash programs do not involve the costs of printing and redeeming vouchers, nor do they involve the bureaucracy necessary to administer the actual transfer of goods and services and to prevent black markets.

- Cash transfers limit the interference with the market system. They do not change the relative prices of particular consumption goods and services as do non-cash transfers. Consumers continue to select market goods and services on the basis of their relative prices.

However, society may wish a particular consumption need to be provided at a level beyond what would occur if the incomes of the poor were raised to some level of adequacy through cash transfers. For example, society seems to value a far more equal distribution of medical care and education consumption than would be effected by just increasing by a modest amount the command of the low-income population over goods and services in general. This is because these particular consumption items are often very expensive relative to income and because they are not universally consumed. Assuming that the market can provide such particular goods and services, vouchers—for several reasons—are generally the most efficient transfer form to provide more of a consumption item than the poor might choose to purchase, had they the cash.

- Vouchers allow the recipient freedom to select the supplier of the goods and often allow freedom to choose among a wide range of goods intended for the particular purpose. Interference with the market place is minimized relative to direct provision by the public sector.

- Vouchers allow targeting of the transfer to those with special needs or tastes. For example, Medicaid payments are made only for those with particular medical needs. Basic Educational Opportunity Grants are given only to those interested in higher education who have been accepted by approved institutions. If such programs were "cashed-out" and the average value provided to all eligible recipients, it would not be sufficient to provide for the high consumption levels of those particular goods or services needed or desired by only a subset of the eligible population. Further, those without the special need would receive an unnecessarily high basic benefit.

- Vouchers involve lower administrative costs in comparison with the direct public provision of goods and services.

Thus, vouchers are appropriate when society wants to encourage the utilization of a particular good or service available in the market beyond the level at which it would be consumed if a greater cash income were available to a recipient, or to provide benefits to recipients that are limited to a particular purpose. However, two things should be noted in connection with these goals. First, to the extent the voucher simply frees cash resources that the recipient would otherwise have spent on that particular good or service, the use of a voucher has not restricted consumption patterns any more than an equivalent amount of cash would have. Second, if the voucher value is sufficiently in excess of what the recipient would otherwise have spent for its designated purpose—such as for food—the worth of the transfer to the recipient is less than program outlays. Often in these cases black markets arise, thereby encouraging and allowing the recipient to convert the voucher into cash.

Vouchers are preferable to cash on efficiency grounds only under the limited circumstances described above, since they involve greater administrative costs and interference with the market and the consumer's freedom of choice. They are preferable to direct public provision of goods and services except under the conditions described below.

Direct public provision of goods and services is appropriate when special characteristics of a particular good or service make it inappropriate or impossible for the good to be supplied through the private market mechanism at a roughly equivalent or lower cost, or when it is desirable to control the exact nature of the good or service being provided—public education is a possible example. Cash or vouchers will obviously not increase command over particular goods and services when these are not available in the private market. And, where the exact characteristics of the good are important, vouchers may not be an efficient way of assuring that these precise characteristics are met. Under these circumstances, direct public provision is probably the only way to accomplish the desired objectives. However, direct public provision involves a number of well-known problems. It should be limited to those cases where it is essential because, of all the transfer forms, it requires the largest administrative costs (relative to benefits received) and may involve considerable waste (recipients of the food distribution program have been known to throw out unwanted commodities).

If the efficiency criteria for the form of transfers that best meet particular consumption needs are applied to the components of the existing welfare system, a considerable reshaping of the components is suggested. Strong consideration should be given to de-emphasis of many programs that directly provide goods or services, in favor of greater emphasis on cash or voucher type assistance. Also, many needs now met through vouchers can probably be met better through cash.[36]

This is easily said, but not so easily done. One reason is that there is a wide range of other considerations besides efficiency that enter into processes that determine the various forms of welfare benefits. These were mentioned briefly earlier, when the impact of the current welfare system was discussed; further elaboration would not serve the purposes of this paper. Suffice it to say that although efficiency criteria cannot (and should not?) be the sole factor in determining the form of welfare transfer benefits, they should play a larger role in any restructuring of the system than they appear to have had in its development. The alterations such criteria suggest appear to be consistent with other reform goals, such as greater administrative simplicity.

Different Types of Cash Programs, Their Forms, and the Trade-Offs Implicit in Their Structure

The government has available a range of programs to provide cash income transfers to members of the low-income population so that they might attain a minimum adequate level of command over goods and services. Noncash transfer programs that meet consumption needs that cannot be adequately supplied by direct cash transfers are not considered here. However, it is assumed that there will always be a need for some such programs (catastrophic health coverage, for example), even if a cash program provides fairly generous and universal coverage. The extent to which it will be possible to eliminate a multitude of noncash programs will be influenced directly by the degree of adequacy and coverage of any cash program. Accordingly, some of the examples included here use what might appear to be a rather high basic benefit level ($4,000 for the proverbial urban family of four); it should be kept in mind that this example assumes that some in-kind programs are cashed out. The greater the extent to which cash basic benefit levels are below this amount, the greater will be the pressure and need for many noncash programs for the low-income population.[37]

It is assumed, in light of the conclusions in the first section, that the objectives of cash programs are to provide adequate benefits in an equitable way at minimum cost in an administratively simple manner without inducing undesirable behavioral responses.[38] Given these goals, all such programs should share one common characteristic: a benefit level conditioned on family size and income. Few would quibble with these as objectives for an income transfer system. However, they do not comprise an exhaustive set of concerns, for policymakers often are worried as well about who ought to receive benefits and under what conditions. Different weights placed upon different concerns have resulted in preferences for different program types.

To see how this happens, it will be useful to begin this consideration of types of programs by describing the simplest and most universal program type, and then examining how the introduction of different concerns and changes in their weighting leads to alterations in program design. Finally, an approximation of our current system, with all of its undesirable attributes, is arrived at.[39] Along the way, most of the programs that have been suggested as possibilities for welfare reform are identified. The more universal programs are considered at some length here; the more categorical ones are considered in detail later. Adopting this approach has two distinct advantages:

- It presents a broad overview of most of the different types of programs available prior to more detailed discussion.

- It helps to clarify what is being relinquished in order to gain something else. An understanding of this enhances the ability of policymakers to select an appropriate balance among somewhat conflicting objectives.

These policy concerns, together with the problems raised by multiple program participation and poor program integration, go far toward defining the present dilemma.

POSITIVE AND NEGATIVE TAXES

The federal income tax is universally applied among the population. But within its structure, forms of tax relief or tax aids are provided that are related to the welfare concept or, more broadly, to income maintenance. These structural features exclude from income tax liability persons below certain levels of income, based on size of family, and provide tax relief according to marital status, age, or disability. Moreover, certain types of income received are excluded from the tax base, and certain types of expenditures are deductible from income, resulting in a wide range of substantial tax subsidies or transfers to the nonpoor.

These tax relief features were adopted to provide equity according to the ability-to-pay principle and to create financial rewards for certain types of behavior. In a conceptual sense, the welfare principle might be the converse of the ability-to-pay principle—that is, people should receive transfer payments according to their ability-to-receive, their need. Accordingly, income-tested transfer payments should be viewed as negative taxes and tax relief from positive taxes should also be viewed as negative taxes (or implicit transfers, also sometimes referred to as "tax expenditures").

Many of the public issues and debates that deal with relief from the income tax and with welfare are related to the public interpretation of the concepts of ability-to-pay and ability-to-receive, respectively.

The personal exemption provisions in the income tax system,

in conjunction with the low-income allowance, ensure that no family incurs a federal income tax liability until its income exceeds the poverty level.[40] This feature of the tax system could be interpreted as a public judgement that no family or person should be required to share in the support of the government until it earns at least enough to provide for its own minimum needs. A logical extension of this principle would imply that the tax system transfers funds to those whose income is below this minimum standard. As we have seen, our present welfare system does this to some extent, but not in a very satisfactory or comprehensive manner.

A UNIVERSAL REFUNDABLE TAX CREDIT

A fully integrated universal tax-and-transfer system, more than any other program type, might achieve the goals of adequacy, simplicity, equity, and absence of undesirable behavioral response.[41] This is accomplished by instituting a "refundable tax credit," which would work in the following way: each person in the country is credited with a yearly grant or credit (say $1,300 per adult and $700 per child in high cost areas). This would replace the existing provisions for personal exemptions, so that all income (other than that taken out of the tax base for other reasons) excluding the grant is taxed. If the family's tax liability exceeds its credit or grant, it pays net taxes; if not, it receives a net transfer.

This program (as is true of all income-tested transfer systems) has the same basic design as the pure negative income tax (NIT), but can be administered more easily. The basic benefit level is the amount of the family's credit or grant. The tax rate or benefit reduction rate is that contained in the income tax system. Income is whatever is in the income tax base. The breakeven point is that income level where the credit and tax liability are equal.[42]

One of the most desirable features of this program is its simplicity and objectivity. No information is required that is not presently on the income tax form, and no independent administrative structure is needed. Instituting a universal tax credit would, of course, substantially add to the administrative burden of the Internal Revenue Service (IRS), but this burden would be insignificant in comparison to the administrative structures that are necessary to sustain the existing income-tested cash and noncash transfer programs. In addition, under a unified tax-and-transfer system, there would be no "welfare population" that could be delineated and stigmatized. Such a system might well be socially cohesive rather than divisive as is the present system.

On the other hand, such a universal tax credit is likely to require substantial changes in the positive tax system, including major alterations in the definition of taxable income and allowable deductions. Because the benefit reduction (or tax) rate related to the credit would be applicable in the tax system, it is expected that the marginal tax rate would be fairly modest. Under a system with a $4,000 credit for a family of four and a 33 percent tax rate over the lower range of income levels, families of this size with incomes up to $12,000 would still be receiving a net transfer. If the goal is general income redistribution, this result is not undesirable and may even generate additional political support. High-income families would be financing transfers to low-income and middle-income families, even though many of those low-income families were not in poverty. However, if the goal is simply to assure that only extremely low-income families are raised to a minimum adequate level of income, the refundable tax credit should be scored for a lack of target efficiency. A program that is "target efficient" in this sense—by raising all family incomes to the minimum standard—achieves its goal with a minimum of spillover (net transfer to those whose incomes are already above the minimum standard).

Thus, financing the refundable tax credit at any substantial level would require a significant change in our present tax structure.[43] Such changes might be welcomed by many, but as a practical matter they would have to be considered a severe obstacle to the institution of a tax credit that would permit the elimination of many present welfare programs.

A UNIVERSAL NEGATIVE INCOME TAX

If it is felt that substantial modification of the current income tax system is impossible, or if the large size of the population that would receive net transfers under a refundable tax credit scheme is thought to be undesirable, the minimum adequacy goal can be approached via a two-part tax-and-transfer system, generally referred to as a "negative income tax." The principles underlying the universal negative income tax and the refundable tax credit are identical: (1) Each family is assured a basic benefit level related to family size and living situation; (2) the higher the income of the family, the less the net transfer benefit; and (3) at some level of income (the breakeven level), the family becomes a net taxpayer instead of a transfer recipient.

A negative income tax proposal, as usually presented, differs from the refundable tax credit proposal in that under a negative income tax, net transfer recipients would be subject to a different structure of tax rates—and possibly income base, filing unit, and accounting period definitions (see Appendix)—than are net taxpayers. Negative income tax proposals usually contain a high constant marginal tax rate (say, 50 percent to 67 percent). Because of this, the size of the population receiving a net transfer is much smaller than under a refundable tax credit with the same basic benefit level so that persons are not simultaneously receiving a benefit and paying taxes. Ideally, the breakeven level of income should coincide with the income that is exempted from taxation in the positive tax system. At this income level, the family leaves the negative tax system and joins the positive tax system with its lower and presumably progressive tax rates.

Thus, a universal negative income tax overcomes two of the possible objections to a refundable tax credit. It does not require major modification of the positive tax system, and it can restrict coverage to the poor and near poor while providing reasonably adequate benefits by levying a high tax rate on the earnings and other income of recipients. With a 67 percent tax rate and a $4,000 basic benefit, a family of four ceases to be eligible for any transfer when its countable income rises to $6,000. This greater target efficiency does not come without cost, for we have kept the complexity of our existing positive tax system and added to it a tax-and-transfer scheme at the low end of the income scale. In order to limit coverage, high marginal tax rates have been imposed on those who are transfer recipients. So, relative to the refundable tax credit, target efficiency has been increased at the expense of significantly increased administrative costs and complexity, and of potentially greater work disincentives. In addition, we have now somewhat separated out and possibly facilitated the stigmatization of a particular population.[44]

THE INCLUSION OF ADDITIONAL CONSIDERATIONS

A refundable tax credit or negative income tax can be universal, as described just above, or categorical. In order to limit costs and preserve popular support, legislative proposals to date have limited negative income tax type proposals to families with children (FAP) or to the aged, blind, and disabled (SSI), thus excluding non-aged ablebodied childless couples and unrelated individuals who may be equally needy.

Similarly, some countries have a categorical form of a refundable tax credit—a children's allowance—which requires considerably less transfers than a universal tax credit and targets the benefits on a most popular group.

By imposing categorical limitations, the administrative simplicity of a universal program is lost and incentives to alter family structure are built into the system. For example, FAP would have created a strong incentive for a couple to have a child. These incentives are undesirable but flow from an attempt on the part of policymakers to positively restructure the present system.

Another critical aspect of a negative income tax is lost as one moves toward a categorical cash transfer program. Both the ability and the desire to tie the program into the tax system (conceptually and administratively) are severely vitiated. Rather than providing a replacement for an eliminated welfare system, then, there is greater danger that the more undesirable aspects of welfare will creep back into the system and that another layer will be added to the present welfare system.

The desire to ensure no diminution of work effort as a result of receipt of transfer benefits and the further desire to provide a strong positive work incentive have led to at least two further modifications to a simple cash transfer program. These are the so-called work-related expense deductions and work requirements. Work-related expense deductions add considerable complexity, individual variation, and inequity to benefit determinations, since their treatment may require a case-by-case review. A work test to implement the work requirement necessitates a large scale administrative operation to determine employability and provide for training, placement, and other manpower and work-related social services.[45] These considerations have led to the highly complex and less-than-satisfactory WIN program, a program within a program.

The concern with work effort has added a further complication: the need for a sizeable establishment to administer a public employment component within a complex income transfer program. (Work requirements, employability, work incentives, manpower services, and public employment are all the topic of detailed discussion in Chapter 3). The Opportunities for Families Program (OFP), added to FAP during its second House consideration, is an example of such an apparatus,[46] as is the Work Administration proposed by the Senate Finance Committee. Many of the functions of these agencies would have been far removed from the administration of an income transfer.

Finally, if policymakers wish to condition benefits on work through means other than public service employment (particularly for intact families), the eligibility of certain demographic groups and their level of benefits can be tied *directly* to working, as in a wage rate subsidy or earnings supplement plan. (These are taken up in detail in Chapter 4.) These require much the same administrative apparatus as noted above, and, in the case of the former, also require more detailed information on earnings and employment. They would also create another overlapping category of recipients, which is undesirable on grounds of administrative complexity and the creation of incentives for changing family structure. On the other hand, these schemes would aid the working poor. The recently proposed British Tax Credit, also described in detail in Chapter 4, represents a rather ingenious method of employing a categorical refundable tax credit to provide benefits to those low-income families in which the head earns at least eight pounds a week. Because the British Tax Credit proposal is administered through the British income tax and withholding system, it minimizes the administrative complexity of an added categorical program. Unfortunately, the complexities of the American tax system make it difficult to adopt an approach similar to the British one.

Another possibility is to limit benefits to those whom society feels are somehow deserving and the coverage of whom will not produce undesirable consequences (like reduction of work effort). The SSI and AFDC programs are examples of this approach. However, in the case of AFDC, there is a clear incentive for two-parent families to split or not to form. Twenty-three states have attempted to meet this problem with the Unemployed Father (UF) option. This, as has been shown, has problems of its own. In addition, there has recently been greater concern that many mothers than are working, could be. This led to the 1967 WIN amendments and then the 1972 Talmadge amendment while FAP was still being debated.[47] All these problems arise from an attempt to further split up the needy population into categories that reflect different social concerns, some dealing with the problem of need and some with anticipation of the recipients' responses to the cure.

So far the discussion has been limited to considerations surrounding the conditions imposed upon the receipt of cash assistance. Quite by themselves these conditions have contributed much to the current complexity of the welfare system. However, there is an additional consideration, which was discussed extensively in the first part of this chapter: the form of the transfer benefit.

As indicated there, other forms of benefits than cash may be justified on grounds of efficiency, but these instances are rarer than the present welfare system might suggest. Several additional considerations play a role in determining the shape of any proposals for a reformed welfare system: the general political acceptability of noncash benefits relative to cash, particularly for coverage of populations where the question of work incentives is at issue; the committee structure of Congress; the desire to restrict recipients' use of benefits to particular purposes; and the effort to serve one or another special interest group. These factors clearly played a strong role in determining the shape of our present system. However, the benefits of constructing a welfare system that takes these considerations fully into account must be carefully weighed against the costs. For as we have seen, the proliferation of noncash welfare programs, each with its own target population, delivery system, regulations, and other characteristics, has contributed greatly to the current "welfare mess."[48]

On the other hand, the political favoritism generally accorded noncash welfare transfer benefits could be used to advantage since this form provides a less controversial means of providing coverage to certain populations. However, if such a tack is pursued (that is, more of an "in-kind strategy" as opposed to a "cash strategy"), careful consideration must be given to which noncash programs should be retained (or created) and how they should be modified in order to better meet the objectives for a welfare system set out in Chapter 1. This is a topic of further discussion in Chapters 5 and 7, where coverage of intact families and the general subject of program interrelationships respectively, are treated.

Conclusions

How the pursuit of particular concerns influences the various proposals for welfare reform has been indicated previously. When pushed far enough, these concerns lead back to the present patchwork system of cash transfer programs, with all of its inadequacies, inequities, inefficiencies, and administrative complexities. All of these problems are further exacerbated by society's decisions to provide many benefits to the low-income population in noncash, rather than cash, form in order to meet needs that require only a minimum level of generalized purchasing power.

A universal refundable tax credit, which "cashes out" many of the noncash benefits, is probably the most straightforward way of accomplishing the delivery of needed purchasing power to the low-income population, consistent with the criteria of an income-tested transfer system as described in Chapter 1. However, it would require major tax reform and may be too redistributive. Given these obstacles, a negative income tax administered by the IRS and partially integrated with the tax system may be preferable. It is more target efficient and can be implemented with fewer changes in the current tax system, although it does entail some additional administrative complexity for IRS and greater concern over work disincentives. Both the refundable tax credit and the negative income tax as described have the potential to replace the welfare system with a substantially different concept and a structure more akin to the tax system.

The imposition of additional considerations leads away from such an elimination of the welfare system to either broad or narrow structural reform of the present system. As relatively greater weight is placed on the objective of target efficiency as it pertains to demographic categories and as additional considerations, such as work requirements and preferences for noncash transfers, are taken into account, the program options available are relatively less successful in meeting the objectives relating to administrative efficiency, equity, and coverage.

In Chapters 4 to 6 some of the approaches to welfare reform that take the work incentive issue and additional considerations into greater account are dealt with in more detail. But first it is necessary to discuss in more depth the work requirement and related issues.

3

The Work Requirement and Related Issues

As noted earlier, concern that employable individuals might choose to reduce their work effort if they are included in an income maintenance program has led to the inclusion of a work requirement in recent welfare legislation. Currently, employable persons receiving AFDC are required to register for training and employment under the WIN program. The Family Assistance Plan proposed in 1969 by the Administration included a similar work requirement. In these instances, the "work requirement" is actually a requirement to register for work or training and to accept a reasonable placement, or risk the loss of benefits. However, if there are no job or training slots available, a nonworking employable person would continue to receive benefits. A more rigorous work requirement would ensure that no benefits accrue unless the employable person were actually working. Several alternative transfer programs in which this more rigorous work requirement is incorporated are discussed later.

After a discussion of the theory and evidence on work incentives, this chapter will attempt to place the work requirement within the context of a number of measures that somehow relate transfer benefits to work effort or at least to the willingness to work. Many feel that such a course is required to preserve the integrity of a transfer program in view of questions of equity among those who work and pay taxes and those who receive transfers. While the evidence presented below suggests that a strong concern regarding the willingness of transfer recipients to work is not justified, some policymakers and other citizens argue that permitting any ablebodied person with no compelling child care responsibilities to receive a significant basic benefit is wrong. In part, this is a philosophical argument. However, this concern raises difficult questions of how to determine who is "employable" and how to decide the best way to implement a work requirement. In fact, the term "work requirement" is a misnomer, since work-relatedness is in fact a matter of degree, represented by a continuum of possible measures that welfare policymakers may choose to utilize.

Work Incentives

In theory, any transfer program (AFDC, FAP, NIT) that includes a basic benefit plus a benefit reduction rate on earnings tends to reduce the incentive to work in two ways. First, the basic benefit raises the income of the recipient. He may feel richer and tend to consume more of *all* goods and services, one of which is leisure. That is, a recipient may choose to use part of his transfer to replace income he previously obtained by working.[49] Such a result has been referred to as a work disincentive. But it must be noted that the transfer recipient need not use the newly "purchased" leisure for "slothful" activity. He may, for example, search for a better job or enter a training program. Evidence from the OEO New Jersey Income Maintenance Experiment suggests that this is, in fact, what blacks have done.[50]

The tax or benefit reduction rate produces a second possible work disincentive. If the recipient has any earnings, then the transfer system's tax rate reduces the amount of the basic benefit he receives in some relation to the amount of his earnings. This tax rate thus reduces the recipient's reward for work. If he works an additional hour at $2, his income no longer rises by $2, as it would have before the transfer system was introduced (abstracting from income and payroll taxes).

An AFDC recipient, for instance, who earns an extra $2 has her benefits cut back by $1.34 (67 percent of $2) over a certain range of earnings, so that her reward for work is reduced from $2 to $.66 as the result of the AFDC tax rate. Since work is less rewarding, it is less costly in terms of forgone earnings to consume leisure instead of working. Hence, there is an incentive to substitute leisure for work.[51]

It should be noted that the conventional economic analysis used to predict the theoretical work disincentive is "static." That is, it looks only at one period in time: the period during which the transfer is received. A more forward-looking analysis would attempt to examine the effects on future employment and earnings of more time for job search and better health and nutrition (purchased by the income transfer), and on other desirable behavior. The long-run disincentive effect may therefore be overstated by static analysis.

This discussion can be extended from the basic benefit and tax rate of one program to a multiprogram world. The cumulation of tax rates has been the subject of much discussion and is generally recognized to be a serious problem. That the basic benefits of different programs also cumulate is less often fully appreciated but the work disincentive from this source is potentially as serious as the tax rate effect.

If the public were not convinced that certain recipients of public transfers would cease to work, or work less, the issue of work incentives would not arise and the principal categorical break within the needy population could be eliminated. But the public is concerned that those poor who are able to work do so. Work has a high place in the American system of values. Not only does this value induce virtually all who are ablebodied to seek work, it produces a distaste for those who do not work. Since work is a social value of the majority, a nonwork environment is undesirable. It is a short jump to the argument that people *should* work, for their own and their family's good.

THE EVIDENCE

According to the latest Census data available (1971), 75 percent of all poor, male family heads worked during the year, and 51 percent of those working worked full time, year round. Of the women who headed low-income families, 41 percent worked in 1971, 18 percent of those working did so full time, year round. Low-income persons who did not work for reasons other than school, illness, or family responsibilities represented only about 5 percent of all poor persons of working age. These data would not seem to suggest that poor family heads have a weak attachment to the labor force. Indeed, given the poor labor market prospects known to face this population group, such data may be surprising for the level of positive attachment they indicate.

Attempts to analyze the work incentive effects of transfer

programs of the negative income tax variety have been of two types—experimental and econometric. In the OEO New Jersey experiment, groups of intact families were put into an income-tested cash transfer system without a work requirement, and their work behavior charted relative to a control or nontreated group. It has been found that reasonably generous plans, in which earnings are taxed at rates of up to 70 percent, result in no significant change in earnings of the family head and in average reductions in hours worked of approximately 6 percent. Econometric estimates based on the behavior of male, prime-age family heads are roughly consistent with the experimental results just cited.[52] It should be noted that all of the evidence cited in this paragraph applies to families living primarily in urban areas. Evidence on rural families covered by a similar experimental program will not be available until July 1974; preliminary indications are that it will be generally consistent with results of the above studies.

The WIN experience with the AFDC population seems to indicate that despite the reasonably high benefits and the relatively high benefit reduction rates faced by large portions of the AFDC population, the desire of female family heads to work is substantial. Widespread research supports the conclusion that AFDC recipients are highly motivated to work, as this quotation indicates:

> The AFDC program includes a wide variety of recipients. For most in our sample, welfare was not a "way of life." They wanted and requested job training which would lead them away from the brink of poverty, but were even more eager for a job. They did not fit the stereotype of the inter-generational poor family with little work experience and no desire to work.[53]

A recent, well-publicized Brookings Institution study showed that the commitment to work among welfare mothers was as strong as (or perhaps stronger than) that among nonwelfare recipients.[54] Another pertinent fact is that throughout its history the demand of volunteers for WIN work and training slots has exceeded the supply.

The econometric evidence on the work response of secondary workers suggests that there is a significant reduction in hours worked in response to high basic benefit levels and tax rates. That is, the aged, teenagers, and married women with husbands present are likely to reduce substantially their work effort if their families are covered by a welfare program. Presumably, the work effort of secondary workers is of considerably less concern than the work effort of prime-age family heads, primarily because of the value placed on nonmarket alternatives of secondary workers, especially school work and home work.

FURTHER DISCUSSION

This is not to imply that there is no work incentive problem. But the evidence suggests that the problem is not sufficiently severe to merit the concern it has aroused. As long as male family heads can obtain some reward from work, the experimental and econometric evidence indicates that their work effort is little reduced by basic benefit levels in excess of those proposed in the FAP legislation. Evidence from the WIN program indicates that most female family heads also have a strong motivation to work outside the home. Nevertheless, despite the documented evidence to the contrary, popular misconceptions about the incentive to work of the low-income population persist. The concern over work disincentives caused by moderately high basic benefit levels and benefit reduction rates is real, and policymakers would do well not to ignore it.

Given this concern, how can work incentives be maximized? Unfortunately, this goal is not easily attained because of conflicting objectives. A low basic benefit level coupled with a high disregard[55] and a low tax rate would preserve strong work incentives. But the lower the basic benefit level, the less adequate the benefit structure is. Furthermore, the higher the disregard and the lower the tax rate, the more benefits are transferred to the near poor relative to the poor. This means that target efficiency is low and program cost high. Thus, judicious trade-offs must be made among basic benefit levels, disregards and tax rates, and the level of the breakeven point. One approach to the problem of conflicting objectives would be to categorize the recipient population, providing high basic benefit levels coupled with high benefit reduction rates (to keep the breakeven point low) for those populations for whom work incentives are a less important concern than adequacy, and somewhat lower benefit levels and tax rates where work incentives are a concern. (In this respect, the perversity of the current system is interesting to note. The SSI population is provided with generous disregards and a 50 percent benefit reduction rate over all ranges of earned income, although there is little concern that they work. In contrast, the AFDC-UF population faces a 67 percent benefit reduction rate on up to 100 hours of work per month, at which point all benefits are terminated.) Unfortunately, if public concern over work incentives results in a high degree of categorization, the efforts to correct many of the undesirable features of the current welfare system will fail.

Work and Welfare: A Taxonomy

The methods of dealing with concern over the work incentives for transfer recipients can be reduced to four basic ideas, which follow:

Work Incentives. As described in the previous chapter, programs are structured so that transfer recipients who work keep a substantial portion of earnings and therefore find work financially rewarding; this implies low benefit reduction rates. (It also should imply low basic benefits; since many welfare recipients face poor earnings prospects, large basic benefits could dissuade them from working.)

Work Registration. As a condition of eligibility for benefits, an "employable"[56] adult must register for work or training and accept a job if offered. Such a provision is frequently referred to as a work requirement and is found in the current AFDC program. Note that work is not, in fact, required.

Work Opportunity. Welfare applicants are given an opportunity to earn, via a public sector job, an amount equal to or greater than a welfare grant. Essentially this amounts to a public employment program. If the monthly wage is equal to the local welfare grant, such a program would be similar to what is called "work relief." At higher wages the term "public service employment" might be used.

Work-Conditioned Benefits. In this case, both the receipt and amount of benefits are tied to working as in a wage rate subsidy or an earnings supplement. (To a significant degree then, public employment, as just noted, is work-conditioned, although benefits may not depend on the amount of work).

Chapter 4 of this paper will describe in some detail the programs noted in the latter two categories. Here the problem of choosing which methods should be included in a welfare system that covers ablebodied adults will be considered. Ignoring the issue of work incentives is neither wise nor politically possible.

It should be clear that only the first option above, the provision of work incentives, does not necessitate a categorization of the population into employable and unemployable persons. In effect, this option accepts whatever work effort reduction is occasioned by the transfer program, assuming that the program's work incentives will be sufficient to avert an undesirably large reduction in work effort, or that, in any event, the costs of attempting to prevent work reduction through other approaches exceed the potential benefits.

Work registration, as in the WIN component of AFDC, does require categorization of the recipient population into those who are and those who are not thought to be employable. Employability, however, is not a straightforward concept. It is a question of who, in some sense, is "able to work." But the answer depends not only on the characteristics of the recipient but also upon the type of work, on the one hand, and the state of the labor market, on the other; for example, the very tight U.S. labor market during World War II pressed into service persons who previously were thought to be unemployable.[57] Disability is also a difficult concept to handle; while some medical dimensions are well defined, disability determinations vary with doctors' philosophies and patients' needs and desires. Purely physical determinations of employability are possible, but these can not be expected to be uniform over time or across persons.

Employability has two further dimensions that must be considered. First, as far as competitive private sector employment goes, employability varies over time and space as a function of quantity and quality of labor supplied relative to that needed. Thus, to the extent that the private sector would play a nontrivial role in employing welfare recipients, the vagaries of the business cycle and its differential regional impact would complicate employment slot planning.

A further dimension relates to the "employability" of mothers of young children. If all the women in question are considered employable, using both physical and economic criteria, the difficult issue of weighing the value of home work against work in the labor market must still be confronted. There seems to be general agreement that mothers with very young children should not be required to work and that mothers with no children under 15 should work, but there is considerable controversy over the cases in between. If mothers with preteenage children are required to work, then there would be pressure on the government to accompany this work requirement with the provision of adequate child care facilities[58] and other work-related social services as well as manpower services and, when necessary, public service employment.

Thus it should be clearly recognized that a system that seeks to categorize the population administratively takes on a substantively difficult task and also a large and costly administrative burden.[59] More important, perhaps, is the effect on those declared employable who can find no job, and are shuffled from office to office.

Since the provision of manpower services has been an integral part of welfare plans incorporating a work registration requirement (the current WIN program and the OFP portion of the Family Assistance Plan, for example), it may be useful to briefly examine the subject. A manpower service is any one of a number of activities that is designed to increase the employability and/or earning power of the person successfully treated. Outreach, counseling, testing, training (institutional or on-the-job), placement, follow-up, and day care are the standard manpower services. Public employment might be considered a manpower service since it combines many of the others and, indeed, is a much less roundabout method of achieving the same goals. However, it will be treated separately below.

The extent to which any cash transfer program incorporates manpower services depends on society's estimate of their efficacy in achieving the program's goals, as well as on the specific nature of the program. The desire to improve the earning capacity of welfare recipients in order to simultaneously reduce their dependency and the tax burden of welfare payments, has in the past led program designers to provide welfare recipients the full range of manpower services. Unfortunately, after the vagaries of the job market are taken into account, there is little hard evidence that argues for the efficacy of manpower services provided to the welfare population.[60] And the less-than-satisfactory experience with the WIN program provides little comfort.

This pessimistic reading of the evidence on manpower services for the welfare population does not mean that their provision should be ended. Such a policy change must wait for stronger evidence than is now available. However, this evidence does suggest that manpower services cannot be counted on to ensure the success of a work registration program and that their application to various subsets of the "employables" should be carefully considered in a cost-benefit framework.

Another important point implicit in most of the discussion of work registration requirements is that the costs, burdens, and potential benefits will vary markedly across demographic groups. Prime-age, male family heads, for example, would, as a group, place a small burden on the system because they are unlikely to enter the work-test system, and if they do, they would not need the most expensive service—day care.[61] Female family heads, on the other hand, are likely to enter the system in large numbers and use virtually all of its services, particularly day care. It seems clear, then, that the cost-effectiveness of a work requirement for female family heads would be well below that for male family heads, a possibility policymakers may want to take into account.

While on its analytic merits, the case for a work registration requirement may be weak, on its political merits, the case may be stronger. If a work registration requirement is chosen, then what remains to be decided is whether to go in the direction of a WIN-OFP work requirement, with a sizeable administrative burden handled by a large bureaucracy, or in the direction of a simpler, work-conditioned benefit type program (see below). With respect to the latter, the difficult questions are, How is a program for the clearly employable to be related to one for the not-so-clearly employable? or How is a new work-conditioned cash transfer program to be related to the existing AFDC program?

The ultimate work requirement is a program that pays no benefits unless the program participant works. This would not be the case with the program variants just examined. Public employment and work-conditioned cash transfers would, however, provide a more stringent work requirement. Both of these variants will be discussed at some length in Chapter 4. Here, some of the trade-offs involved in each of these programs and also among the four methods of relating work and welfare are noted.

With the exception of the Depression Era, there has been great reluctance to establish large scale public employment projects in the United States. This may seem paradoxical in a country so wedded to the work ethic and with such concern about both welfare and unemployment. Apparently, the desire to minimize the size of the public sector and the known expense and administrative difficulty associated with public employment has contributed strongly to this situation. To some extent this reluctance still exists, but it is clearly breaking down. The evidence comes in two forms. First, all recent welfare reform proposals incorporated substantial sums for public service employment.[62] Second, the "work relief" idea—requiring certain welfare applicants to "work off" their welfare grant—has been getting a great deal of attention recently. Work relief, of course, is simply public employment at relatively low wage levels. It requires job development, placement, and supervision as does public employment by any other name. Since work relief has never been used on a large scale, it is not clear if large numbers of useful public jobs for low-skilled persons can be found or if these jobs will lead to private sector or regular civil service employment.[63] Current state efforts should be carefully evaluated. A primary question is the extent to which the jobs created for welfare applicants are new jobs. If welfare recipients simply displace other workers, little gain is achieved by the program.

Conditioning benefits on the earnings of low-income workers, as in a wage rate subsidy or an earnings supplement, is a technique to provide income assistance to the working poor. Since program benefits are zero if hours worked are zero, wage rate and earnings subsidies minimize concern regarding work incentives. Such programs have a serious flaw, however: those who cannot find jobs will through no fault of their own receive no benefits. And presumably they need income assistance at least as much as the working poor. Obviously, in such cases, public employment is the only way to ensure income assistance *and* continued work effort. It should also be noted that determining who is eligible for the work-conditioned benefit and who is not, as well as obtaining the wage and hour information to make payments, imply an administrative structure of some size and complexity.

Finally, a distinction should be made between reducing hours worked and quitting work entirely. Work requirements of various forms may be effective in reducing the incidence of the latter, but are unlikely to affect the former.

Conclusions

The discussion in this chapter has attempted to get behind the rhetoric on work requirements and to provide some insight into the exact nature of the choices. First, a review of available evidence suggested that the negative impact of income-tested cash transfer programs on work effort does not appear to be excessively large, at least for the groups of greatest policy concern. However, if policymakers desire to relate benefits to "work," techniques are available. The work registration technique is not a "work requirement," but it can serve a useful, if limited, purpose in answering public concern about the welfare system's attitude toward the ablebodied recipient. It has been argued that categorization on the basis of subjective employability determination is expensive and when no jobs are forthcoming, such categorization is destructive of work registrants' attitudes toward work and toward the welfare system. Similar categorization and administrative structures are required by public employment and by work-conditioned transfer programs.

The problem seems to be that of finding a way to ensure that the system does not appear to be handing out benefits to any and all ablebodied adults who apply. This is presumably what is meant by preserving the integrity and equity of the system for the overwhelming majority of those who do work and pay taxes. One of the principal problems with the work registration system, which carries over to any employability determination, is its case-by-case method. If hard and fast predetermined categories were set up (and the inherent difficulties in such a process have been noted) and if these categories were enforced *only* if jobs or training slots were available, the system would be simpler.[64] For such a system to work, the categories would have to be determined so that there would be little debate over who is, in fact, "employable," in the sense of being immediately job-ready. Classifying women with children less than 15 years old as not employable is one example of the type of determination that would be necessary under such a system. In addition to such conceptual difficulties in establishing definitive categories, many persons would not agree with the categories and thus would not feel the system was equitable.

Viewed in this way, the work requirement is seen to be less of a "you have it or you don't" proposition and more of a way to avoid the worst abuses of a cash transfer system while minimizing administrative burdens and cost. The most straightforward way to do this, via public employment, is probably the most costly and burdensome. Enforcing strong work requirements via work-conditioned transfers has the serious weakness of excluding from assistance those unable to find employment. Thus, while some would argue that such policies may be necessary to ensure passage of income transfer legislation, the very important costs of these policies must be borne in mind.

4

Work-Conditioned Programs

One of the objections often made to any income maintenance program that provides an amount of supplementation inversely related to earned income is that some members of the population who are able to work may choose to reduce their work effort. Public concern over the poor population's incentive to work has been one of the stumbling blocks to passage of an income supplementation program for the working poor. This same concern led to the imposition of a work requirement on employable AFDC recipients.

In Chapter 3 of this paper, however, a good deal of evidence was presented to show that public concern over the poor population's incentive to work may be ill-founded. The evidence indicates that the poor population has a strong commitment to the work ethic. Even when their reward for work is small due to high benefit reduction rates, their commitment to work is strong. Despite the lack of evidence to support the fear that the welfare rolls will be swollen by "freeloaders" if welfare coverage is offered without a work requirement, political considerations may make it necessary to impose some sort of work requirement on those who are expected to work. In this chapter several programs that incorporate a work-conditioned benefit structure are examined; these programs pay out benefits only if the recipient is actually working.

Before proceeding, it should be noted that many of these work-conditioned programs are merely outlined and still await full analysis. It is useful to recall that it took many years and much intensive scrutiny of negative income tax plans before the full impact of the crucial issue of program interrelation and accounting period were recognized. A principal complication with regard to work-related programs is uncertainty about how they interrelate with programs for the nonworking poor and the single parent AFDC population. This issue is ignored here unless the plan discussed deals with all family types, but will be taken up later.

Cash Transfer Programs

WAGE RATE SUBSIDY

A wage rate subsidy (WRS) augments the recipient's hourly wage. The more hours worked, the greater the subsidy. More significantly, if no hours are worked, no benefits are paid. It is in this sense that the wage rate subsidy is said to be "work-conditioned." Typically, wage rate subsidy plans establish a socially determined target wage. Some percentage, called the subsidy rate, of the difference between the target wage and the worker's market-determined rate is added *to* the market wage rate. The goal of the wage rate subsidy is to increase the income, via wage earnings, of low wage workers. Another goal is to increase employment: it is generally expected that the subsidy will increase the labor supply to some extent and reduce the cost of labor to employers. (It is implicitly assumed that the wage rate subsidy more than compensates the worker for his reduced market wage.) The potential employment-creating effect of the wage rate subsidy is welcomed for obvious reasons, particularly because it would, by bidding down wage rates, make low skilled labor more attractive to many employers. This feature is quite similar to the benefit attributed by some to a differentially lower minimum wage for teenagers. And for the same reasons, it would be likely to encounter similar opposition. In addition, because the WRS might bid down market wage rates, it would invite charges of subsidized "sweat-shop" employment.

The feature of the wage rate subsidy that has attracted the most favor is its greater apparent work incentive effects compared to a negative income tax. Earnings from an additional hour's work are supplemented rather than taxed; the greater reward for work should induce greater incentive to work. However, there are a number of problems associated with a wage rate subsidy. Increases in wage rates (as opposed to hours worked) are positively taxed; thus there is some reduced incentive for making investments to increase one's hourly wage rate. Since the subsidy can be maximized by underreporting wage rates and overreporting hours, or by receiving compensation in nonpecuniary form, there exists an incentive for employer-employee collusion. The problem to be corrected is low family income, but the WRS pays benefits based on an individual worker's wage rate. Hence, the target efficiency of a simple wage subsidy is low, since many low wage earners (about 80 percent) are members of nonpoor families. Target efficiency could be improved by limiting the wage subsidy to family heads and by varying the size of the subsidy in response to family size. Thus, greater target efficiency can be bought at the cost of increased administrative complexity. But, even for a simple wage subsidy, the administrative problems are not trivial. For example, how are non-straight-time hourly earnings (such as tips and fringe benefits) to be handled? How are benefits to be related to family need over time? Should benefits be paid directly to the worker or through the employer? To date, there has been no programmatic experience with a wage rate subsidy. Such a plan was, however, explicitly proposed in the Senate Finance Committee's version of H.R. 1.

EARNINGS SUPPLEMENT

An earnings supplement (ES) differs from a wage rate subsidy in that the benefit structure is based on total earnings rather than on the hourly wage rate.[65] The typical simple form of an earnings supplement pays the worker a certain percentage of his earnings up to a specified earnings level (the "kink point"). Below the kink point, an extra dollar earned results in more than an extra dollar of income to the worker, increasing the reward to work. Above the kink point, the supplement is reduced gradually to zero as earnings become higher. Because the benefit is reduced as earnings increase in the income range above the kink point, earnings are implicitly taxed, just as they are under a negative income tax. When the supplement is reduced to zero, participation in the earnings supplement program ceases.

Thus, an earnings supplement can be divided into two distinct parts: (1) the subsidy phase, where the supplement increases as earnings increase and work is rewarded with more than a dollar of income for a dollar of earnings; and (2) the tax phase, where the supplement is reduced as earnings rise and work effort is taxed. It should be noted that in the second phase, while additional earnings are "taxed," a positive supplement is still paid to the family. The second phase, as noted, is identical to a negative income tax in its effect.

For those who are already working, the earnings supplement could either increase or reduce their work effort. While the subsidy phase may promote work effort, the necessarily accompanying tax phase discourages work effort. However, like the wage rate subsidy, the earnings supplement provides no guarantee or basic benefit to those who do not work. Persons who earn nothing receive nothing. Hence, both programs provide a strong incentive to enter or to remain in the labor force, and, compared to an NIT, much stronger disincentives to labor force withdrawal.

Since the earnings supplement is based on earnings, rather than on hourly wage rates or hours worked, the potential for collusion that exists with the wage rate subsidy is reduced. The need for earnings figures only, makes administration of the earnings supplement simpler than the wage rate subsidy. Earnings, moreover, are much closer to income, the really key variable, than is the wage rate. These are rather important and fundamental distinctions between the two approaches to providing cash transfers to the working poor. It should also be noted that the earnings supplement can be dependent on total family earnings or total earnings of all adult members, unlike the WRS, which has to relate to individual earnings. This makes it simpler to target the benefits more efficiently on low-income families, especially if nonearned income serves to reduce the size of the supplement.

If the central goal of improving work incentives in income maintenance programs is to encourage persons to work more hours, then an earnings supplement might be less effective than a wage rate subsidy. Because an earnings supplement is based on earnings, which is the product of hours worked and the hourly wage rate, it treats increases in earnings due to more hours worked or a higher wage per hour identically. A wage rate subsidy, on the other hand, encourages increases in hours worked much more than do higher wage rates. Because the supplement takes into account only total earnings (unlike a WRS), it can be criticized for aiding individuals with high wage rates who work few hours. This objection might be met if the supplement were limited to family heads, because the incidence of part-time work in that group is low. Alternatively, some substantial minimum hours of work could be required before a part-time worker were eligible for supplementation.

Other problems relating to the earnings supplement are

similar to the technical problems involved in designing and implementing any income maintenance program. For example, should the benefit be calculated on the basis of total family earnings? How should unearned income be taxed? What sort of accounting period is appropriate and feasible? How can benefits be made sensitive to family size? These problems notwithstanding, in a number of significant aspects the ES has advantages over the WRS as a method of establishing a clear tie between cash benefits and work effort.

Like the wage rate subsidy, the earnings supplement has not been tried in practice, though a form of supplement was reported out by the Senate Finance Committee.[66] In that version, called a Tax Credit for Low-Income Workers with Families, a supplement of 10 percent would be paid on earnings up to $4,000. For earnings in excess of $4,000, the tax or benefit reduction rate would be 25 percent. Consequently, some benefit would be paid on all earnings up to $5,600, after which program participation would cease.

WORK-RELATED NEGATIVE-INCOME-TAX-TYPE PLANS

Many who have been concerned with reform of the welfare system favored the universal NIT concept because of its presumed efficiency. Other concerns, however, led first to the administratively complex and cumbersome FAP-OFP form of the NIT in H.R. 1, and ultimately to its legislative demise. Since the major problem concerned work incentives, those still favoring the basic NIT approach have attempted to revise certain aspects while preserving some of the desirable structural features of the NIT. Thus, a class of plans, some of which are not fully work-conditioned in the sense that the WRS and ES are, has come into public discussion. It seems convenient to call these, work-related negative-income-tax-type plans, even though they are categorical in their coverage and generally not integrated with the tax system. Three such plans will be examined here: the British Tax Credit plan, the Mega plan, and the Aaron plan.

The British Tax Credit Plan. The British plan, as proposed in a recent British Green Paper, is very simple in form and administration.[67] The plan, mentioned in Chapter 2 as a specific form of a refundable tax credit, would apply to persons who regularly work for an employer, to beneficiaries of social insurance programs (unemployment compensation, sickness and injury benefit, maternity allowance, and invalidity pensions), and to recipients of a national insurance retirement pension or widow's benefit (equivalent to Social Security beneficiaries).

In order to qualify for the tax credit, a person must have an income of at least eight pounds ($20) per week—all beneficiaries of the national insurance programs listed above would be included. The plan would cover about 90 percent of the adult population and their dependents. The largest excluded group is the self-employed. Also excluded are welfare recipients who have no attachment to the labor force and would be covered by a separate program.

The credit is a function of family size and income. Employers apply a flat tax rate of 30 percent on earnings. The tax credit is then added in. If the tax is greater than the credit, the difference is a tax deduction from earnings. If the credit is larger, there would be a net addition to the pay check. The appropriate government agency would do a similar calculation for national insurance recipients, taxing benefits at 30 percent and then applying the credit. Income from other sources—interest on savings and dividends, for example—would be taxed at the source, again at the rate of 30 percent. This differs from the current practice in the United States of taxing the unearned income of income maintenance recipients at 100 percent.

An important asset of the British scheme is its administrative simplicity. All payments are made directly by employers without the need to file monthly or quarterly reports. Because the flat 30 percent tax covers virtually all persons, there are no year-end adjustment problems.[68]

It should be noted that the Tax Credit proposal integrates the positive tax system with the national insurance system. But it is primarily an income supplement for low-income wage earners and national insurance beneficiaries. Conventional welfare and social service programs remain in place to assist those persons in need of income support up to the subsistence level.

The British Tax Credit is work-conditioned in that only those who receive at least eight pounds per week, either in earnings or national insurance benefits, are eligible. Thus, one must be working or must have worked sufficiently in the past to qualify for national insurance in order to be eligible for the tax credit. The poorest of the poor must be covered with more traditional welfare programs.

The fact that most of the British population is covered by a flat 30 percent tax rate is an important feature of the plan, one which adds considerably to the simplicity of the tax credit. This feature alone may make the plan politically infeasible in the United States, since it would entail significant changes in the income tax structure.

The Mega Plan. In its 1972 plan for comprehensive simplification and reform, the Department of Health, Education, and Welfare proposed for all families a variant of FAP, which has come to be called the Mega plan.[69] It provides no benefits to those considered able to work ("availables"), but does give a basic benefit to their families based upon the number of members who are not "available." "Available" adults are able to earn, tax free, an amount equal to the breakeven level of income for a single individual. The plan thus improves the work incentive features of a general negative income tax plan by lowering both the tax rate for availables and the guarantee for their families. A 50 percent tax rate is suggested after the initial earnings disregard. Earnings derived from public service employment would not enjoy this initial disregard but would be taxed immediately at 50 percent. Thus, not only does the Mega plan provide availables with a strong incentive to work, but it also makes regular labor market employment considerably more attractive than public service employment. Other possible features might include subsidies to private employers and "last resort" public jobs in order to assure a job for anyone willing to work. These are not essential to the plan design and could be modified within the basic structure.

Instead of imposing a rigid "work requirement" on an individual, the Mega plan attempts to improve the incentive to work and to provide opportunities to find a job. However, it explicitly categorizes the population by predetermined employability definitions. All ablebodied male heads of intact families are considered to be "available." A problem that must be faced here—or in any income maintenance program that separates out "availables" for different treatment—is how to deal with involuntary unemployment or temporary disability. Will income maintenance be provided for the unemployed and temporarily disabled by social insurance programs, or will methods for rapid reclassification of "availables" have to be devised?

The recommendation in the plan is that heads of single parent families be considered "available" only if they have no children at home who require day care. In effect, this relieves the government of the massive day care and public service employment requirement implicit in the work requirements in H.R. 1 and in the Senate Finance Committee's plan. (But, like the present

WIN program, mothers who volunteer to participate would be able to avail themselves of manpower training, public service employment and day care to the extent that funds existed for it.) As social mores dictated and the budget permitted, the "available" categorization could be extended down through mothers with school age children, perhaps including those with the fewest children first.

An interesting strength of the Mega plan is that, although it does create categories ("availables" and "nonavailables") to allow a differentiation that promotes work incentives, it does so in a way that retains a common program structure for all families, thus reducing the incentive to alter family arrangements. The rest of the family members are treated the same whether or not the "available" member is included. Thus, this plan retains much of the strength of an NIT for families.

The Aaron Plan. This plan was proposed by Henry Aaron of The Brookings Institution.[70] Families are ensured a basic benefit level ($2,400 for a family of four) even if no member works. However, the plan, which is complex, is constructed so as to maximize all of the relevant incentives to work.

Increases in earnings due to increases in hours worked and to increases in hourly earnings are treated differently. Since the author feels that the Congress and the public are principally concerned with incentives to work more hours, as opposed to working at higher wage rates, the marginal tax on increased hours is held to between 0 and 30 percent, depending on the actual wage rate and the hours worked. Wage increases, on the other hand, are taxed at 60 percent. In this regard, the plan is structurally similar to a wage rate subsidy grafted into a negative income tax.

The plan creates no categories; all families are treated alike so that there are no undesirable incentives to alter family structure. However, two sets of tax rates would be needed, as well as data on both wage rates and hours worked, in order to administer the program. Implementation of the program would combine the administrative problems of both the negative income tax and the wage rate subsidy.

Public Employment

In some respects, public employment is the most straightforward way to implement a work-conditioned transfer. Strictly speaking, a transfer exists only if the value to society of the goods or services produced by the public employment is less than the cost. Many have argued that, given the unmet need in social and community service areas, the net social benefit would be significant. If such is the case, it is reasonable to put to work those who currently receive transfers and who could produce needed social services. Clearly, taxpayers would be better off with the production of socially needed services than without them and, given society's view of the intrinsic value of work, so would the recipients.

The counterarguments stress the low productivity of the welfare population, the (frequently underestimated) cost of public job creation, the difficulties of administration, and the undesirability of a significant expansion of the public sector. Experience with public employment has not been sufficient to determine whether the first three of these concerns are serious enough to preclude implementation of a large public employment program. The fourth concern is principally a matter of ideology. However, due at least in part to the strength of this ideology, an incongruous situation has arisen: we wish to tie transfer dollars to work effort, but fail to provide the necessary number of jobs.

The arguments against public employment are examined here, but without going into great detail and without providing a definitive evaluation.

- That members of the welfare population have few labor market skills is to some extent self-evident. If this were not the case, they would earn reasonable private sector wages. But to base an argument against public employment on this fact ignores the proven existence of numerous barriers to work and of labor market discrimination against females and blacks. Even if this population has a low level of skills, should this situation be considered permanent, or does society have a responsibility to alter the skill levels of the population? While previous examination of the success of manpower services gives no cause for great optimism, the evidence is not strong enough to write off this population.

- Public employment would be more costly than an equivalent cash transfer equal to the program salaries if the value of public employment output is ignored. This is because of the overhead involved–plant and equipment, supervisors, and the like. Furthermore, the better the program is in providing training and earning opportunities, the more expensive it is. Using an overhead rate of 30 percent (which is probably conservative) and an hourly wage of $1.60 for 1,500 hours per year, a public employment program for one million persons would cost $3.12 billion, transferring $2,400 to each participant.

- It is difficult to ensure that public employment, or indeed any job creation efforts not accompanied by an expanding economy, would add to the net pool of employment. To varying degrees the newly created jobs might duplicate ones that already exist or would have come into being anyway. It would take considerable administrative ingenuity to ensure that the displacement effect is not significant.

- In addition to the problems discussed previously, the administrative difficulties of public employment abound. A partial listing would include the following: if sufficient numbers of slots were not provided, rationing (categorization) devices would have to be designed; wage and personnel policies would have to be promulgated; because the supply population for public employment would no doubt ebb and flow by location with changes in the private economy, the size and composition of the work force would vary geographically and over time, thus complicating such procedures as staffing and project selection.

These arguments, together with the bias against enlarging the public sector, make up the not unimpressive case against public employment. For these reasons, no programs requiring massive public service employment have been considered in this document. However, there could be a role for public employment for employable heads of low-income families, at least on a time-limited basis. Even if a strong work incentive were built into the transfer system, public employment might be viewed as a tool for providing employment for those who would be liable to face long-term unemployment. How much public employment it would be desirable to provide at any one time, should remain an open issue, but the need would certainly increase with the strength of any work requirement and the aggregate unemployment rate.

In general, three broad types of public employment may be distinguished: public service employment, public works employment, and "make work" or "work relief" employment. (1) Public service employment generally refers to work in the provision of "soft services," like counseling and referrals. Included in this category would be work as a "paraprofessional" and as an "aide." (2) Public works employment, which is generally capital intensive, usually includes work on publicly financed buildings, parks, roads, and dams, with the jobs being in construction or maintenance. (3) "Make work" or "work relief" employment is defined not by the kind of work performed but by the fact that it is labor of some kind supplied in a public job as required in order to receive welfare benefits. Frequently, agreement to take any jobs that are available also fulfills this requirement. In this analysis, public employment work is explicitly distinguished from jobs in the regular civil service. While this is in accord with general practice, it is not necessarily desirable because it reinforces the distinction between welfare recipients and others.

Revenue sharing can be used as a vehicle for providing public jobs, as in the Emergency Employment Act of 1971. A problem here concerns the ability of state and local governmental units to efficiently use shared federal revenues. A related technique would involve federal subsidies to subnational units of government for the express purpose of hiring labor for public service jobs. The House version of H.R. 1 had such a provision, as does WIN, with the subsidy phasing out over a three-year period.

Public works employment, requiring a relatively skilled labor force, is less appropriate for the welfare population than the other types of public employment. On the other hand, public-works-type jobs are generally higher paying and more respectable than the jobs welfare recipients can usually find. This, in fact, illustrates part of the dilemma facing the designers of public jobs for welfare recipients. The better the job, in terms of salary, working conditions, and future prospects, the greater the cost of providing a job slot. And the more expensive the slot, the fewer the number of slots that can be created within budget constraints.

The California Work Experience project (CWEP) is an operating variant of a public employment work relief program. It is designed to provide work experience for employable AFDC recipients in public service assignments. Participants are drawn from the pool of WIN registrants for whom WIN job or training slots are not available at the time. CWEP participants receive no compensation beyond their AFDC grants. Assignments are typically from 8 to 10 weeks in duration and involve half-time work (80 hours per month).

Perhaps the principal objective of CWEP is to control the size of the welfare rolls. There are two ways in which the program might accomplish this objective. First, it provides a deterrent to potential applicants for public assistance who are employable. It is assumed that such individuals, faced with the prospect of involuntary public service employment, will make an extra effort to find employment before they apply for AFDC transfer payments. Second, it is hoped that the program will enhance job prospects in the private sector for employable AFDC recipients, thereby reducing their dependency on public assistance. CWEP provides the individual participant with job experience and a record of successful employment that can be used as a reference to other employers. It is implicitly assumed that job experience and references are at least as important as skills in finding employment. If a job applicant has a record of satisfactory performance at a public service assignment, a prospective private sector employer can be assured that the applicant meets minimal requirements for punctuality, work discipline, and satisfactory supervisor-employee relationships. Evaluation of the CWEP program after it has been operating for a longer time will permit an assessment of both the benefits and the problems of such an approach to public employment. At this time no adequate evaluation of the program appears to be underway.

With any public employment program, a set of policy trade-offs exists. Given a long time perspective and the desire to ensure permanent private sector employability of welfare recipients, public employment jobs should provide training and supervision and ensure private sector counterpart jobs. The first two of these objectives—provision of training and supervision—are costly and will thus reduce the number of slots. The more the number of slots falls below the number of persons who are required to work and are unable to find private sector jobs, the less meaningful a work requirement becomes. Ensuring a private sector counterpart to a public job is apt to incur the disfavor of business and labor groups and may not add to the total job pool but may simply displace workers in the private sector. The alternative is to provide employment that is of little value either to the recipient in terms of skills acquired or to the public sector in terms of services provided.

Other Alternatives

PAYROLL TAX RELIEF

Unlike the income tax, the Social Security payroll tax is regressive; low-income families pay a much higher proportion of their income in payroll tax than do high-income families. The payroll tax is a flat rate levied on all earnings up to $10,800; no personal exemption or standard deduction is allowed.[71] The result is a tax that bears heavily on low-income earners because wages make up a large portion of their total income and the total amount of their wages is below the payroll tax ceiling. For high-income groups, the payroll tax drops to an insignificant percentage because wages and salaries constitute a smaller proportion of total income, and wages above the ceiling are exempt from the payroll tax. Payroll taxes are a much greater burden to low-income families than income taxes. Indeed, a four-person, single earner family with earnings up to about $12,000 a year pays more payroll tax than federal income tax.[72]

If Social Security contributions are viewed like other taxes, then tax relief to low-income workers is justifiable, because the contributions are currently regressive and not based on ability-to-pay criteria. At the extreme, payroll taxes could be eliminated altogether, with all Social Security benefits financed from general revenues. A less extreme measure would use general revenues only to compensate—partially or fully—low-income workers for the payroll taxes they pay. In either case, the principle that personal contributions are necessary to establish eligibility for later benefits might be vitiated, when compared with the present system, although the employer's share would presumably be retained. Also, eligibility would still be based upon a previous earning history.

But many people do not think of the payroll tax as a tax; rather, they regard it as an insurance-like premium that gives them or their survivors a vested right to later benefits. This view of the Social Security system as contributory and self-financing is probably a major reason for its great popularity relative to other existing transfer systems.

The issue of payroll tax relief is not clear-cut. The ability-to-pay principle, which argues for tax relief, is in conflict with the contributory principle, which has been the ideological core of the Social Security system from its inception. While payroll tax relief would remove a burden from the segment of the low-income population that is making an effort to help itself, it should be kept in mind that tax relief is insufficient by itself to alleviate the poverty of the working poor. A worker with three dependents and earnings of $4,100 a year would get, at most, an extra $239.85 a year in disposable income due to payroll tax relief. Workers with less earnings, and hence more need, would get an even smaller increase in disposable income due to payroll tax relief.[73]

WAGE BILL SUBSIDY

A wage bill subsidy is paid to employers on the basis of their labor costs for certain types of employees. Its purpose is to induce firms to hire more of the subsidized labor than they would in the absence of the subsidy. This result is obtained, in theory at least, by the government's reducing the cost of labor to the employer, the amount of cost reduction being the subsidy.

A wage bill subsidy could be administered by the Internal Revenue Service as yet another part of the tax system. However, some agency such as the Employment Service or the Welfare Department would have to certify certain workers as eligible.

While the wage bill subsidy is often presented as an alternative to the work-conditioned cash transfers discussed previously, it cannot be considered a good substitute for them. Since the subsidy goes to the employer and not the employee, it cannot be used to ensure a transfer of a given amount to the target population. It need have no effect on the earnings of those in the target population who are already employed.

Further, recent experience with the WIN program indicates that very little increased employment of the target population can be expected. Under the WIN program, employers are allowed a tax credit of 20 percent of the wage cost of their WIN-certified employees. It was hoped that this credit would create job openings for AFDC recipients, but employer response to the subsidy has been minor. Even had there been a sizeable employer response, the result would not necessarily have been desirable since it might have been a simple redistribution of an unchanged total unemployment level, with subsidized low skill workers replacing unsubsidized low skill workers.[74]

In sum, the wage bill subsidy does not appear to be a substitute for cash transfers and may not even be a helpful complement.

5

Coverage of Intact Families

The cash public assistance programs, AFDC and Old Age Assistance (OAA),[75] were designed primarily to support the incomes of unemployables. The assumptions that directed the designers of the Social Security system in the 1930s were that the labor market would provide jobs to persons with employment potential and that earnings from employment would be sufficient to provide an adequate level of consumption. The social insurance system was thus designed to enable persons with a labor force attachment to weather temporary spells of unemployment and to provide income support for retired persons, widows, and the disabled. The AFDC and OAA programs provided benefits to the remainder of the population.

As pointed out in Chapter 1, the labor market has not fulfilled its promise, and the coverage of the social insurance system is inadequate. These shortcomings are particularly acute for intact families with children, a population that depends primarily on earnings from employment for its consumption needs and that is largely excluded from eligibility for cash public assistance benefits. The available data for this population show that labor force participation is no guarantee against poverty. Seventy-five percent of all poor, male family heads worked during 1971; half of those who worked, worked full time for the entire year. Thus even full-time employment did not provide an adequate income to a large number of families.

The receipt of public transfer income has relatively little

impact on this population in comparison with its antipoverty impact on the aged, disabled, and female-headed families with children. Sixty-two percent of the posttransfer poor families headed by a non-aged, ablebodied male received no transfer income at all in 1971. The remaining 38 percent remained in poverty despite the receipt of public transfer income. There were over 7.1 million persons in this population group, more than in any other principal demographic subgroup in poverty.

The cash public assistance program has clearly not altered its fundamental categorical structure to reflect these realities. The extension of coverage to poor intact families with children is supported by several arguments.

- Despite extensive labor force participation, this population lives below the level of adequacy, with the consequent physical and psychological hardships that this implies.

- It is inequitable to provide benefits to female-headed families and to deny them to male-headed families in equal need, particularly when many of the male family heads are employed but have lower incomes than some welfare recipients.

- The recognized needs of intact families were a major factor in the creation of the many different specialized noncash programs that have become part of the transfer system and that have contributed to its problems. Providing for this group could help in moving toward a coherent system.

- Extending benefits to intact families would significantly reduce the existing incentive that encourages families to organize themselves in ways related to eligibility requirements.

The arguments for extending coverage are thus fairly strong. One argument against it is that such benefits would occasion a substantial withdrawal of work effort by recipients. However, this position is not supported by the available empirical evidence, as has been shown earlier in this paper. The other major argument against providing benefits to this population is that it would be too costly. While more analysis of the costs of the various options is required, if the extension of coverage is matched by a reform of the existing programs, and the elimination and consolidation of programs where appropriate, the fiscal requirements for new money would be somewhat reduced. For example, cashing-out certain in-kind programs, such as food stamps, would provide substantial resources to finance welfare reform. Furthermore, because most intact families have at least one employed family member, the average benefit per family would be modest. Consequently, the total cost of extending coverage to intact families would be comparatively low. In considering the FAP proposal, it was determined that the net additional cost of providing benefits to the working poor with the $2,400 FAP basic benefit level and cashed-out food stamps would be on the order of $1 billion.

The remainder of this chapter explores the program alternatives for providing more adequate income support to intact families. The discussion focuses on the program alternatives described previously and reviews their applicability to this particular population.

The Refundable Tax Credit and the Negative Income Tax

A refundable tax credit or a universal (or near-universal) negative income tax plan could provide the most adequate coverage of both single parent and intact families and could result in the elimination of many parts of the present welfare system. These programs are also characterized by relative administrative simplicity compared to the others that will be considered here. At the same time, neither of these two alternatives may be acceptable because the coverage may be regarded as too broad or because they do not take sufficiently into account the widely held notion that public assistance benefits should be related somehow to work effort.

The Mega Plan, FAP-OFP, AFDC-UF

If greater attention is to be paid to issues such as the work requirement and manpower services, there are several program options that meet this need and still provide more adequate coverage.

The Mega Plan, for example, meets the work incentive issue by allowing a large range of earnings to go untaxed, setting a relatively low marginal tax rate (50 percent), and providing no benefits to an employable head of a family. Thus there is a strong monetary incentive to work.

FAP-OFP could also be considered an option, although it should be more carefully integrated with the rest of the welfare system than it was in its last revision.

An important benefit of these near-universal approaches (in addition to their universality) is that they can supplant some of the existing welfare programs, thereby streamlining administration. It should be clearly understood, however, that any program that requires an employability test will be more difficult to administer than a program that does not. The extent of administrative complexity will largely depend on the nature of the work test. The registration of employables for work or training is relatively straightforward. However, the actual provision of manpower services and related social services, such as day care and counseling, is more complex, while operating a public service employment program introduces an entire new set of administrative complications.

An alternative to an entirely new program that could still lead to a more common NIT-type coverage for all families, would be to modify and expand the AFDC-UF program. Basically, this would entail defining eligibility in terms of income only and mandating a UF program in those states that do not now offer it.[76] Then within this program, reforms of the type that are suggested for AFDC in Chapter 6 of this paper could be instituted, which would move AFDC and AFDC-UF together toward most of the objectives embodied in FAP. This would significantly alter the nature of the AFDC-UF program. If, on the other hand, certain program features such as eligibility conditioned on unemployment were retained, the program would have relatively little impact on most of the working poor.

Earnings Supplement, Wage Rate Subsidy, Wage Bill Subsidy, Payroll Tax Rebate

This set of program options is even more strongly work-conditioned than the programs described above.[77] Benefits are provided only to persons who work; eligibility is thus contingent upon employment. This means that a significant number of the intact families that would have been aided by the programs described in the previous section (Mega, FAP-OFP) would not be covered by these programs, even though these families may have a strong labor force attachment. Seasonal workers, workers experiencing a lay-off, and the temporarily unemployed, for example, would receive no benefits when not working. While unemployment insurance or other programs—General Assistance or food stamps, for example—may provide income support to some of these families, many of them would not be covered by any program, particularly in times of high aggregate unemployment.

Two things ought to be considered if one of the range of options in this section were adopted to supplement the incomes of the working poor:

- The systems (primarily social insurance) that provide support for intact families with a head who is not employed for the entire year should be strengthened.

- There should be judicious use of job-creating activities for those whose only impediment to employment is the inability to find a job.

The same objectives could be achieved through a more universal program, with the added advantage that administration would not be so cumbersome.

An additional shortcoming of these strongly work-conditioned programs is that none of them deals as directly as the programs described in the previous section with the problems created by the differential treatment of single parents and intact families. Work-conditioned programs help to reduce the disparity of treatment between the two groups, but do so by setting up still another overlapping program structure without abolishing or subsuming any existing ones. These program options thus receive high marks for dealing with the work issue but low marks on coverage and administrative simplicity.

In-Kind and Mixed Cash-In-Kind Approaches

Another approach to better coverage of both intact and single parent families would lean heavily on in-kind benefits. It would recognize that the administration's new health insurance proposal would provide adequately for the health needs of this population and that a combination of basic education grants and educational loans could be appropriately expanded to allow fully for the vocational and other educational needs of participants (thus greatly reducing the need for the provision of institutional manpower training by the federal government). In addition, the food stamp program would provide for food needs. Some sort of income-tested housing voucher could also be provided to all families. Since these two vouchers are near-cash substitutes that represent purchasing power over "basics," when provided in tandem they would essentially provide income maintenance to the eligible population. A variant of this approach would be some mix of cash and in-kind benefits that, taken together, would provide expanded coverage of the low-income population with more or less adequate benefits. The primary advantages of an in-kind approach are the following:

- It would not require the development and submission to Congress, and passage by Congress, of a new "welfare reform" proposal, with all the attendant problems, but would rely basically upon separate pieces of legislation.

- Although food and housing vouchers are little more than disguised cash assistance, they are far less controversial than cash assistance. Thus, they could be extended to all families without categorization.

The primary disadvantages are the following:

- It would be impossible to create an effective benefit structure through this approach that exactly parallels AFDC. The horizontal inequities and accompanying incentive for changes in family composition would still exist, although to a lesser degree than at present.

- The problems involved in appropriately integrating all the in-kind programs would be considerably compounded beyond what would be the case if major reliance were put upon a reasonably adequate universal cash program. A further elaboration of these problems appears in Chapter 7.

- While passage of a universal cash assistance program might be exceedingly difficult because of the many component pieces, it might also be difficult to obtain

> Congressional approval of an in-kind strategy, including the integration of the separate programs. It could well require a length of time extending beyond the life of any one administration.

Summary

A major issue of welfare reform is who should receive benefits. In this chapter the arguments for extending cash coverage to intact families were reviewed. The basic arguments turn on the need to bring these families' consumption expenditures up to an adequate level and to treat both single parent and intact families equitably. The program options examined ranged from those providing universal or near-universal coverage of the low-income population (tax credit, NIT, Mega) to more narrowly defined categorical programs that provided income support only to employed persons (earnings supplement, wage rate subsidy).

As one moves along the spectrum from the universal to the categorical, the administrative requirements become more complex and problems of equity are likely to arise. Furthermore, when compared to an NIT program providing universal coverage, the programs that make employment a condition of eligibility (such as an earnings supplement or wage rate subsidy) are relatively ineffective antipoverty devices although perhaps highly desirable on other grounds.

6

Coverage of the AFDC Population

In previous chapters of this paper a variety of welfare reform options were discussed, ranging from programs that provide universal coverage to the low-income population, such as a refundable tax credit or NIT; to those that focus more narrowly on the employable poor population, such as a work-conditioned variant of the NIT; to those that extend benefits exclusively to employed persons, such as an earnings supplement. A universal NIT or refundable tax credit (with or without a work test) could supplant the existing AFDC program if the benefits were set at a high enough level. Unless the federally established minimum basic benefit[78] were set at a level of adequacy (which by implication varies somewhat by geographic region), some form of supplementation would be required in many states. FAP, for instance, gave states the option to supplement the federal benefit of $2,400 for a family of four. Thus, if the benefit levels in a universal program were set below a basic level of adequacy in certain states, special provision for the AFDC population would be required.

Programs that provide benefits only to persons who are employed will overlap with the existing AFDC program. The 1971 AFDC study showed that almost 14 percent of the AFDC population was employed at the time of the survey. Thus, while an earnings supplement or wage subsidy would not be a substitute for AFDC, coverage would overlap for working AFDC recipients. Program design and administration must take account of this potential duplicate coverage.

In short, it is likely that any welfare reform option will require, at least in the short-run, special provision for coverage of the AFDC population. One purpose of this chapter is to highlight the issues involved in program integration of this group.

In addition, this chapter addresses a set of issues related to improving the existing AFDC program. The discussed improvements in the AFDC program are aimed at making the system more manageable by introducing management controls and uniform procedures and by consolidating programs and functions. Two important effects of this approach could be the elimination of many of the abuses that are found in the present system and the elimination or diminution of many of the inequities that characterize the existing system.

Many of the changes discussed are included to highlight their interrelatedness and to emphasize that they are part of the reform effort. Given the long gestation period for any major reform, regulation changes consistent with overall policy and welfare reform goals should move ahead so as to facilitate the implementation of a new system.

In the first part of this chapter, the issues related to coverage of the AFDC population under the various reform options are reviewed. This discussion centers on two issues: state supplementation, given a universal or near-universal income maintenance program; and the integration of AFDC with an overlapping categorical program for employed persons. In the second part, the possibilities for change of the existing program are explored under six headings: adequacy of benefits; standardization of the program; improvements in work incentives; integration with other programs; federal-state relations; and administrative and procedural changes. The second section deals with the existing AFDC program on a level of detail far more specific than any other section of this paper.

Providing for the AFDC Population Under Welfare Reform

STATE SUPPLEMENTATION

If a universal income-tested cash transfer program were instituted, it would establish a national minimum benefit. Given budget constraints, it would be highly unlikely that a welfare reform that extends coverage to the working poor and sets a national income floor would provide benefits at a level close to that of food stamps plus AFDC in the high benefit states. FAP's $2,400 for a family of four, for example, was below the payment level in 30 welfare jurisdictions (as of July 1972). Furthermore, it would probably be below the subsistence level in many states.[79] Assuming AFDC benefits should be high enough to provide adequate incomes to families with no other source of income, it would be necessary for some states to supplement the basic national benefit. A number of policy issues are raised; the most important are listed below:

- Who should be eligible for supplements?
- On what basis would the level of supplementation be established?
- Should there be incentives to encourage supplementation, for example, federal cost-sharing in supplements?
- What controls, if any, should be placed on the supplement to ensure that work incentives are preserved; that is, what is a permissible tax rate on supplements?
- Would limits be placed on a state's financial liability (a "hold harmless")?[80]
- What agency should administer the supplements?

Each of these will be discussed briefly in turn.

Eligibility for State Supplements. Since states would probably not be in a financial position to supplement the benefits of the newly eligible working poor population, supplements would probably be restricted to persons meeting AFDC eligibility criteria.

This means that inequities between intact and single parent families would be lessened, but not eliminated. The inequities could be eliminated only by setting benefits at the same level for both family types. However, this would not be feasible if there were budget constraints and if benefits for persons with no incomes would have to provide a subsistence level of support.

The Level of the Supplements. Should state supplements be tied to current AFDC benefit levels or should the level be established in a manner that takes into account both interstate and intrastate cost of living differentials? As pointed out in Chapter 1, present interstate differences in benefit levels are only partially based on cost of living differences: they are also related to states' ability and desire to pay more. If state supplements were keyed to cost of living differences, AFDC benefits would be increased in certain states and possibly reduced in others. The issue is further complicated by the absence of state or regional cost of living indices on which to base grant differentials. The establishment of such indices (or their equivalent) must precede the rationalization of differences in benefit levels between states and regions. The possible role of a housing voucher in this regard was noted in Chapter 5.

Incentives for Supplementation. Should the federal government share in the responsibility for setting benefits at adequate levels by providing for federal participation in state supplemental benefits? The trade-off would be to put the same amount of federal funds into raising the basic national benefit. This would provide more fiscal relief to the states and, possibly, make state-funded supplementation on a voluntary basis more likely. A more complete analysis of this trade-off would be useful in determining federal responsibility in this area.

State Supplements and Work Incentives. The problem of cumulative benefit reduction rates and other undesirable program interactions was discussed earlier. In order to preserve work incentives it would be necessary to ensure that the structure of state supplements be consistent with program goals.

Fiscal Relief. A welfare reform program might increase the caseload for state supplements because of the publicity attending enrollment efforts for any new program and the possible changes in certain eligibility rules that might extend coverage. Should states be required to supplement those cases, and should some limit be placed on the extent of their financial participation? Both FAP and SSI had financial "hold harmless" provisions for the states that froze state expenditures at a level equal to expenditures at some earlier date. A similar provision would probably be required in any new reform proposal.

State or Federal Administration. The basic reform program could be administered by the federal government. While federal administration of state supplements would avoid the existence of two administrative structures serving the same population, it would raise a number of other kinds of administrative problems. State supplements would undoubtedly have categorical coverage, which means an additional eligibility determination would be required to identify the subset of persons who are eligible for state supplements. The need to accommodate the different benefit levels and, possibly, eligibility rules would also complicate administration. The complexities of intergovernmental relations when program-operating responsibility is delegated by one level of government to another would also be faced.

If, however, the key program parameters of the state supplemental programs were defined to be the same as those in the federal program and if identifying the population eligible for state benefits were a simple by-product of the federal operation, then most of these barriers to federal administration of the state program would be removed. The experience with the SSI program may tell us whether the political realities permit such simplification of existing programs.

On the other hand, a new cash program for all families could be administered by the states, even though more heavily financed by the federal government than the present AFDC program. Further discussion of the relative merits of state vs. federal administration of income maintenance programs is contained in the next section under Federal-State Relationships.

AFDC AND AN EARNINGS SUPPLEMENT PROGRAM

It was pointed out above that the institution of a categorical program expressly for employed persons would overlap with the AFDC population. The earnings supplement is chosen in this discussion to illustrate the considerations involved.

The integration of the two programs would be complex. To avoid pyramiding benefits, the benefits of one of the programs would have to be counted as income in the other. Since both programs have a work incentive structure, the benefits from one of them could offset the benefits in the other, dollar for dollar. There is an additional complication in that at some income levels in certain states[81] the earnings supplement would provide larger benefits than AFDC. At that point, it would be critical to ensure that an AFDC recipient be transferred to the earnings supplement program. One way to ensure that would be to enroll all working AFDC recipients in the earnings supplement program. This is clearly inefficient, since those persons would relate to two different agencies (assuming separate administration of the two programs). On the other hand, to design a system that would switch people from one program to another at some specific point would require a highly sophisticated management information system. The problems are not insurmountable, but the program design must take into account the interaction between the benefit levels of the two programs.

Other obstacles to integrating the programs could arise from differences in the definition of the eligible unit, the treatment of earnings of other family members, the treatment of unearned income and work-related expense deductions, and the accounting period.

In summary, the integration of AFDC with an earnings supplement or other program for employed persons would be a complex task. It would involve adding another categorical program and compounding the complexity of the existing system.

Refining the AFDC Program

This section of the paper is written under the assumption that considerable time will be required to reform the existing welfare system. It therefore presents a set of improvements that can be made within the structure of the current program, dealing not with the broad issues of possible refinements but with specific details.

ADEQUACY OF BENEFITS

The data presented in Chapter 1 showed that despite the receipt of transfer income, many persons remain in poverty. The low level of AFDC benefits in certain states contributes to this problem. For example, 37 states paid less than the full basic needs standard, as established by the state, in July 1972. In the 18 states with payment maximums under $200 per month for families of four, the average payment standard was $142 or approximately $1,700 per year, 40 percent of the poverty line. While participation in several programs must be considered when assessing the economic well-being of welfare recipients, such participation is uneven, with some recipients doing relatively well and others receiving benefits from only one or two programs. Taken together, low AFDC benefits in some states and uneven participation in other income support programs mean that many recipients remain below the poverty line.

Establishing a national minimum AFDC benefit would bring

increased benefits to many AFDC recipients who still live in poverty despite their welfare status; it would provide benefits to other poor families who are currently eligible for AFDC but receive reduced benefits because of a payment maximum in certain states; and it might extend coverage to other families currently ineligible for assistance in the low benefit states.

It can also be argued that the establishment of a national minimum benefit reflects a more appropriate role for the federal government in an income assistance program than it plays at present. This view holds that the federal government should be more concerned with ensuring that all categorically eligible recipients receive at least a subsistence level income regardless of where they live in the country rather than with matching the payments of states to recipients with incomes well above subsistence level simply because those states are wealthier or have different attitudes toward welfare.

A national minimum benefit could be established in a variety of ways. The differences in benefit levels among and within states could be made more equivalent to cost of living differences. This would eliminate one of the horizontal inequities that exist in the present system. Or, as noted earlier, such cost of living differentials could be effected through a housing voucher system rather than through the cash assistance program.

The antipoverty impact of a modest national minimum benefit would be most dramatic in rural states in the South and West. Establishing a minimum for AFDC families without providing comparable cash assistance to intact families could, however, provide strong incentives for family splitting. Mandating AFDC-UF would provide benefits to families with unemployed fathers not covered by UI, thereby reducing incentives for unemployed fathers to leave their families so that the families could become eligible for AFDC. However, as pointed out earlier, the AFDC-UF 100-hour-per-month work limitation is a strong work disincentive, as is the need to be unemployed before initial eligibility for AFDC-UF can be established. (The possibility of eliminating the 100-hour work limitation is discussed below.) Thus, if AFDC-UF is mandated in its existing or in an only slightly modified form in the effort to minimize family instability incentives, the resulting work disincentives could cause some persons to withdraw from the labor market in order to obtain or retain AFDC-UF eligibility.

These interactions, with their undesirable effects, inevitably result when eligibility categories are defined on a basis other than economic need or some condition not directly related to a person's ability to earn—old age or disability, for example—or on a basis that permits persons to alter their behavior to fit the category. These problems can be avoided only by extending income maintenance benefits to all low-income families.

The institution of a national minimum also should be accompanied by establishment of uniform program characteristics, which are described below. However, it is not necessary to establish a national minimum benefit before proceeding to standardize the program.

STANDARDIZATION OF THE PROGRAM

Since the welfare jurisdictions have a large degree of latitude in defining AFDC, the program actually consists of many different programs. If one takes the position that income maintenance programs should be uniformly administered throughout the country, the current system must then be viewed as inequitable since regulations and administrative practices are significantly different around the country. It is also extremely difficult to alter the current system because somebody or some political jurisdiction will inevitably be made worse off by the change. This will act to inhibit the changes described here, as well as any more fundamental change.

Instituting Flat Grants. As pointed out earlier, the determination of eligibility and the calculation of benefits is an exceedingly complex process. The result is a system that, resting on the decisions of caseworkers, is arbitrary, demeaning to the recipients, and subject to many errors. Instituting flat grants would reduce errors and improve equity. As noted earlier, a number of states have opted for some variable of a flat grant system, a trend that will continue even if flat grants are not mandated by regulation.

Work-Related Expenses. There is also wide variation among states in the treatment of work-related expenses. One result is that persons with incomes well above the poverty level continue to receive AFDC benefits if the recipients have high work-related expenses. This means that in certain cases AFDC recipients have incomes higher than people not on welfare who work full time. The introduction of a standard nationwide work-related expense deduction would help control this problem. It would also reduce administrative problems involved in determining actual work expenses and might be more equitable since it would provide equal treatment to all the employed. On the other hand, a standard work expense would be disadvantageous to those with above-average work expenses.

An alternative approach would be the elimination of all work-related expense deductions on the grounds that employed persons not on welfare do not have that advantage. One effect of this change would be to remove the relatively favorable treatment the present system provides to persons with low earnings: after all the disregards and deductions are subtracted from gross earnings, AFDC participants have little or no income to reduce benefits. Whether recipients actually perceive this effect, and base employment decisions on it, is unknown. However, the expenditures involved in reimbursing work-related expenses could also be used to reduce the benefit reduction rate in the program. The trade-off can be readily ascertained, and a small study of the program and fiscal issues would be valuable.

One final point. The reimbursement of work-related expenses operates to keep effective tax rates at levels that preserve work incentives. Therefore, it should be emphasized that reducing or eliminating the work-related expense reimbursement should be considered only in conjunction with other efforts to preserve work incentives, such as control of high cumulative benefit reduction rates from multiple program participation. Ignoring the problem would mean that cumulative benefit reduction rates could easily exceed 100 percent in many cases.

A legislative proposal to eliminate the reimbursement of work-related expenses (other than child care) in favor of a flat $60 deduction has been introduced to Congress.

Incapacity. A two-parent family with an incapacitated father is eligible for AFDC. Since the states define incapacity within broad limits, the definition varies from state to state. The introduction of a standard definition would eliminate differences in treatment among states.[82]

Assets. There are wide differences in the amount of real and personal property a person may have and still be eligible for assistance. A national standard would eliminate the inequities that result from these interstate differences.

Definition of the Eligible Unit. Differences also exist among states in the definition of the assistance group. Thus some states include unborn children while others do not; some include caretaker relatives and second parents (for incapacity and UF cases) and others do not. Other variations also exist. The definition should be standardized to the greatest extent possible. Definitions of the assistance unit that vary among overlapping programs are discussed below in Chapter 7.

IMPROVEMENT OF WORK INCENTIVES

The disincentive effect of notches was illustrated in the first part of this paper. Leaving aside the Medicaid notch[83] on the assumption that the planned national health insurance program would eliminate it, two other disincentives are dealt with here. In addition, the relationship between AFDC and manpower services is discussed.

Extending AFDC Eligibility to the Breakeven Point. One way of improving work incentives in the AFDC program would be to extend benefits to the breakeven point, rather than cutting them off at the needs standard. At present, eligibility is determined by comparing income to the needs standard. Once eligibility is established, income can rise well above the needs standard because of the work incentive features of the program. This leads to anomalous situations where ineligible people can temporarily withdraw from the labor force, become eligible for AFDC, then resume employment and retain AFDC eligibility.

Extending eligibility to the breakeven, makes sense only when work expense deductions are standardized. If this is not done, every person would have a unique breakeven that would be subject to change if there were a change in work-related expenses. A unique breakeven would mean that eligibility could change if, for example, a recipient were no longer required to purchase a uniform for work, a mother were to have a new child care arrangement that cost less, or a recipient were transferred to a job location that costs less to reach. The administrative complexities and potential eligibility errors are strong arguments against this approach. If a standard breakeven income for determining eligibility were established for each family size, there would still be families who actually broke even at higher or lower levels, depending on the proportion of their income that was unearned and hence taxed at 100 percent.

This change would, however, be costly to implement. It would also exacerbate the existing inequities between single parent and intact families by making more single parent families eligible for assistance.

Eliminating AFDC-UF Notches. Twenty-three states and the District of Columbia have an AFDC-UF program. The 100-hour-per-month work limitation and the exclusion of persons collecting unemployment compensation make it one of the best examples of a poorly designed program. To recommend that it be abolished, however, would merely shift the problem completely to the states, which would have to deal with the needs of such families through General Assistance.

Eliminating the 100-hour limitation on employment would be an obvious step in improving the incentive structure of the program. This would, however, greatly dilute the categorical nature of the program because it would extend eligibility to large numbers of low-income families. The 100-hour limitation could be liberalized (at one time the limit was 35 hours per week), but a notch would still exist. Further, the closer the limitation is to full-time employment, the greater the inequity between low-income families not on welfare and welfare families.

One inequity could be removed by extending eligibility to families receiving unemployment compensation. Another option would be to alter the Unemployment Insurance program so that it would serve a larger role in replacing income lost because of unemployment. It is unlikely, however, that UI benefits would ever be large enough to provide subsistence incomes to the largest families because UI is explicitly designed as a relatively short-term partial income replacement program with benefits based on the beneficiary's former wage rate. It is not designed to provide a subsistence level of income.

If AFDC-UF were made available in all states and benefits were extended to persons eligible for UI benefits, this would lessen some of the inequities that characterize the present program. At the same time, the work disincentives that accompany the program, particularly in states with low average wages, might cause some persons to withdraw from the labor force.

If the 100-hour-per-month work limitation were also removed, the program that would result would closely resemble FAP.

Thus, we find again that work disincentives and inequities seem to be part of the very fabric of some categorical programs. Attempts to eliminate them prove impossible if the categorical nature of the program is to be maintained. In short, certain aspects of the "welfare mess" are the direct result of the structure of the welfare system itself.

Assessing Work Requirements and Manpower Services. Chapter 3 and the discussion of public service employment in Chapter 4 dealt extensively with considerations of relevance here. There it was shown that while attitudinal surveys indicate employable welfare recipients are generally highly motivated to work, the empirical evidence indicates that only 14 percent of them are employed. However, experience to date indicates that the program cost and administrative complexities introduced by a work requirement that is strictly enforced appear to considerably outweigh any possible benefits. Also it appears that not much can be expected from WIN and other manpower programs. The major problem is simply a lack of jobs paying adequate wages for the population in question. To the extent that the government is willing to provide public service employment for welfare recipients, this can be overcome, but extensive use of such employment has severe problems of its own that are not yet well understood.

In short, this is an area where the problems are likely to remain unsolved in the near future, but the federal government should continue to experiment with innovative approaches to job training and creation in the hope that macroeconomic policy can steer us towards a sustained high employment economy.

INTEGRATION WITH OTHER PROGRAMS

In the first part of this paper it was explained how the existence of many programs led to high benefit reduction rates and administrative complications. Even if the categorical nature of AFDC remains unchanged, there are a number of ways in which the program interrelationships can be rationalized. Chapter 7 describes the techniques for integrating one program with another. Mention will be made here only of the integration of AFDC and SSI, and AFDC and social insurance programs.

AFDC and SSI. The SSI program provides income support to aged, blind, and disabled persons (including disabled children) and essential caretakers. This means that certain families will receive benefits from both SSI and AFDC when either a parent or child in an AFDC family is blind or disabled. (A limited number of aged persons may also be caretaker relatives for dependent children.) It makes little sense to have two agencies relate to the same family for essentially the same reason. A study of the fiscal and programmatic impact of extending SSI coverage to dependent relatives of SSI recipients will be undertaken as part of a larger look at coverage of the disabled population.

AFDC and Social Insurance. Two types of relationships now exist between AFDC and the major social insurance programs (OASDI and UI). Benefits from OASDI are taxed at 100 percent for participants of both AFDC and AFDC-UF programs, while UI benefits are taxed at 100 percent for AFDC participants and preclude AFDC-UF eligibility for unemployed fathers. This treatment of social insurance benefits by the welfare system results in situations in which AFDC recipients eligible for social insurance benefits are no better off for this eligibility, and the unemployed who receive AFDC-UF benefits receive more than the unemployed who receive UI benefits.

If these situations are perceived as undesirable they can be partially corrected by two changes in the way these programs interrelate: eliminating the receipt of UI as an obstacle to eligibility for AFDC-UF and taxing social insurance benefits at less than 100 percent in the AFDC programs. One possibility in the latter regard would be to treat social insurance benefits like earnings and apply the $30 disregard plus the 67 percent benefit reduction rate. Such benefits can be viewed, after all, as a form of deferred compensation.

Such a change does have the undesirable consequence of reducing the target efficiencies of welfare benefits, since it would direct more to families with higher incomes. However, this is the price that must be paid to move toward a situation in which recipients of social insurance benefits are better off than those who are on welfare without either earnings or social insurance benefits. Of course, as long as some groups, such as most fathers of intact families, are categorically excluded from receiving cash assistance, some welfare recipients who are not working will be better off than excluded persons who either do work or receive social insurance benefits or both.

FEDERAL-STATE RELATIONS

This section begins with a review of the ways in which state and local management capabilities can be improved. Next, federalization of the welfare system is discussed. Since the pros and cons of this option are quite familiar, the discussion is brief. The last issue addressed is whether the federal-state financial sharing formula should be altered.

Improving State and Local Management Capabilities. Assuming no change in the roles of the federal and state governments in AFDC, are there any possibilities for improving the management of the program? The issue can be expressed in another way—what techniques can be used to hold the states accountable for the quality of program administration? Some possible approaches are listed below:

- The quality control program can be improved and expanded.

- Federal matching for administration could be increased to the same level as social services (currently, administration is a 50 percent match, while services are matched at 75 percent).

- Federal assistance, either financial or technical, could be provided to states for the computerization of their welfare system. Efforts to maintain the compatibility of such systems would be a necessary part of that activity. An automated data system would provide welfare managers with an information system and client-tracking capability that would greatly facilitate program management.

- Technical or financial assistance in staff training and management improvement could be provided.

- Special studies and analyses designed to provide more empirical evidence about the nature of the AFDC caseload could be supported with research funds.

- Innovative demonstration projects that test new administration techniques and procedures could also be supported.

Federalization of Welfare Administration. Many of the changes discussed above involved making the determination of eligibility for assistance a more straightforward and objective process and making the welfare system as a whole more uniform in terms of both program design and administrative practice. If these are viewed as desirable goals, one way to achieve them would be to have the federal government administer the income maintenance part of the welfare system.

The arguments for local control generally hinge on the notion that persons at the local level are best able to exercise the judgements required in a program based on a case by case evaluation of need. If the welfare system moves to a more objective mode of administration, the need to make case-by-case subjective judgments no longer exists, except in short-term emergency assistance programs.

Experience with the existing system shows that state and local governments have often been forced for financial reasons to interpret federal regulations in a fashion that served their budgetary interest rather than welfare policy. Federal regulations have resulted in additional costs to the states, while certain state actions (witness the claims for federal matching for social services) have resulted in additional costs to the federal government. Too often, efforts at saving money are dissipated on finding ways of shifting costs from one level of government to another. The result of sharing decision-making power between levels of government is that neither level is in a position to control the program effectively. Federalization would obviously resolve this problem, because responsibility and authority would be lodged at one level of government.

Whether such a controversial change can be made will depend in large measure on agreement that a good income maintenance system is one that is uniformly and objectively administered throughout the country and that provides a level of support that is adequate and equitable. On the other hand, it is probably not feasible to have a federally administered program that attempts to take into account a large number of interstate and intrastate differences. As pointed out above, the economies realized by having one administering agency could well be lost if uniform benefits and procedures cannot be adopted.

Relating Federal Cost to State Fiscal Effort. The design of the federal-state cost-sharing formula is an issue that is not directly related to any particular administrative configuration. As long as there is cost sharing, the formula may take a number of forms.

The current reimbursement formula takes into account state per capita income as it relates to national per capita income. The formula, however, does not take into account the level of state fiscal effort with regard to AFDC. As a consequence, high reimbursement rates are provided to states that put forth low fiscal effort. Fiscal efforts range from 0.648 percent of personal income in the District of Columbia, which receives 51 percent federal match, to 0.048 percent in South Carolina, which receives 82 percent federal match.

Even if no other changes were made in AFDC, a more equitable reimbursement formula could be designed so that state fiscal effort as well as per capita income would be taken into account.

ADMINISTRATIVE OR PROCEDURAL CHANGES

The management of the welfare system could be improved by introducing certain procedural or administrative changes.

Monthly Reporting. Recipients often are overpaid or underpaid because changes in income and family status are not reported on a timely basis. In fact, many states do not even have forms on which recipients can report such changes. Consequently, changes are often not reported until the six-month regular redetermination, which itself is often significantly delayed.

If all recipients were required to report their income and family size each month, such overpayments and underpayments would be minimized. Monthly reporting requires data processing capabilities beyond those currently in place to handle the increased volume of reports. There is no doubt, however, that such a system is feasible.

Given the cost of such an investment, the benefits and costs of monthly reporting should be carefully evaluated before proceeding. This can be accomplished by conducting a small scale field test of the procedure.

Accounting Period. The accounting period is, at first glance, a misleadingly simple issue. It is the time period over which income is measured for the purpose of calculating the level of benefits due a recipient. However, a closer analysis reveals that the particular accounting period strongly influences several elements:

- The size of the caseload and thus the cost of the program.
- The responsiveness of the system in adjusting to changes in income.
- Whether or not families of the same size and with the same annual income are treated equitably.

The existing welfare system is based on a monthly accounting period. Only current income and monthly available resources count for eligibility determination; previous income, no matter what its level, is not considered. Compared to an accounting period of longer duration, this approach results in relatively greater program costs, relatively greater responsiveness to income changes, and relatively less equity—since a family with a steady but low income may receive nothing while a family with a fluctuating income pattern may be eligible for benefits part of the year. For example, in a program with a $3,000 guarantee for a family of four and a 50 percent benefit reduction rate, a family with an income of $6,000 spread evenly over the year will receive no benefits, while a family of four with $6,000 of income earned in the first six months and no income during the rest of the year will receive full benefits for the last half of the year.

An annual accounting period would result in relatively more equity, relatively lower costs, and relatively less responsiveness to income increases and decreases. Thus in the above example, neither family would receive benefits, although how a family of four lives for six months with no income is not immediately apparent. There is, then, a spectrum of choice, moving from least cost-least responsive-most equitable to highest cost-most responsive-least equitable.

It is clear that neither end of the spectrum offers a desirable program option. If the purpose of an income maintenance program is defined as the provision of basic income support in cases where a family is unable to secure enough income to live at some minimum level, then the need for a highly responsive system becomes relatively less significant. This means that the income replacement function—that is, assistance needed when there is an interruption in an accustomed income flow—would continue to be handled by other programs, such as OASDI and Unemployment Insurance. (This obviously does not apply to AFDC applicants who have not been in the labor force. The way their eligibility could be established is explained below.) Assistance in times of crisis or emergency would also have to be provided through another program, such as General Assistance or Emergency Assistance. Placing the problem in this context leads to the selection of an accounting period that lies toward the end of the spectrum where equity is maximized, that is, an accounting period of more than a month. This can be achieved by employing a technique, called a carryover, that takes previous earnings into account. This approach would require the establishment of a more adequately funded (that is, with federal cost-sharing) General Assistance or Emergency Assistance program to assist persons who have little or no current income or resources and who are ineligible for AFDC because of past earnings.

Note that if the AFDC accounting period were changed, the past earnings of a now absent spouse would have to be treated in some fashion, probably by assigning all past income to the absent person. Only current income and resources of the family and past earnings of the spouse remaining with the family would be considered. Any accounting period change would affect only recipients who receive income other than AFDC, and then only when it fluctuates.

Such a fundamental change should not be undertaken without further study to assess the impact of various accounting period options on costs, caseloads, and recipients.

Strengthening the Responsibility of Relatives of Minor Children. Many AFDC cases have their genesis in the failure of parents or other responsible relatives to meet obligations to minor children. The federal government could require states to maintain active units for the purpose of obtaining support from absent parents. In addition, model state legislation could be developed, which might include these elements:

- Provisions to strengthen the legal responsibilities of absent parents.

- Authority for rigorous enforcement of such laws within the judicial system.

- Provisions that would require absent parents to make child support payments directly to state income maintenance agencies. This should be a deterrent against skipped, late, and partial payments. It also removes the need to adjust an AFDC grant if a support payment is late, skipped, or only partially paid.

Such measures are not costless to implement. The costs and benefits of these procedures should be carefully monitored through time to ensure that they are cost-effective.

Summary

To summarize, there are several possibilities for improving the AFDC program, even if no reform of the categorical program structure is undertaken:

- Establish a more adequate benefit level.

- Make procedures and program definitions more uniform throughout the country.

- Improve work incentives.
- Rationalize program interrelationships.
- Improve state and local management capabilities.
- Federalize the administration of the program.
- Make certain administrative or procedural changes designed to improve program management.

7

Program Interrelationships

To some extent, this whole paper has been about how different components of the transfer system relate to each other. This section will more explicitly examine the program interrelationship issues—on two levels. First, the place of transfers in American society will be reviewed broadly. Second, a number of technical adjustments that could be utilized to improve the present system will be examined in the abstract. This will require going over some ground covered in earlier sections, but from a different and perhaps additionally useful perspective.

The Social Transfer Account

The current welfare system is composed of a somewhat haphazard array of programs that were individually created and structured over a long period of time in response to an apparent multiplicity of problems. To some extent the needs for food, housing, medical care, and cash assistance are different and separable needs. However, these needs are also evidence of one common problem—insufficient income to meet certain consumption standards. The existence of many different income and consumption support programs must be explained in part by a real desire to control the expenditure of transfer dollars. Yet it may also be explained by the historical timing of both the manifestation of social concern for a particular need and the availability of resources to meet that concern, without any significant continuing analysis or control of the growing system as a whole. The federal government annually redistributes a huge amount of purchasing power. It may be sensible to view this amount as a whole—as a "social transfer account"—and to examine (1) the overall impact of the transfer system and (2) within that system the distribution of dollars to different needs. It is then appropriate to evaluate the adequacy and rationality of the current system. Is the present transfer system sufficient? Is the present distribution desirable? Are the forms of transfer rational and efficient?

For the moment, analysis will be limited to the basic cash, food, medical, and housing assistance programs that are targeted primarily on the low-income population. Concentrating on these major programs will facilitate insights into these questions, insights that should be equally relevant to many other income-tested programs. A more universal analysis using the "social transfer account" framework would include all instruments of income transfer, including the social insurance system, the income tax system (the "tax expenditures" implicit in the structure of exemptions and deductions), and non-income-tested expenditures for education, health, housing, and other purposes. These transfers are of relatively greater benefit to the middle-income and upper-income brackets, but they also provide substantial assistance to the poor. However, this paper will deal only with a portion of the "social transfer account"—the income-tested income transfer system. Table 10 is an estimate for the "core" of the income-tested portion of the social transfer account for FY 75.

Whether or not this $21.8 billion is sufficient is a subjective question, and the answer is at least partially dependent on the definition and the relative importance of the adequacy goal. One conceptual standard of adequacy is the substantial alleviation or elimination of income poverty. In 1972 there were 24.5 million persons in families with incomes below the relevant poverty thresholds, which are well below the median family income.[84] Since the transfer system has not eliminated poverty, the system could be judged inadequate. However, adequacy can also be defined separately from the general level of poverty, related instead to specific population subgroups. The question of adequacy merges with the question of the desirable level and extent of income redistribution. Recent data suggest that even the large growth of cash transfers in the last few decades has neither significantly altered the relative distribution of income nor

TABLE 10: ESTIMATED INCOME-TESTED PORTION, SOCIAL TRANSFER ACCOUNT, FISCAL YEAR 1975

Program	*Billions of Dollars*	*Percentage*
AFDC	4.5	21
Medicaid	6.2	28
Food stamps	4.0	18
Housing	2.3	11
SSI	4.8	22
	21.8	100

Source: The Budget of the United States, Fiscal Year 1975.

significantly reduced the poverty gap.[85] The lowest and highest quintiles of the population, and the 60 percent in the middle of the income distribution, split up today's economic pie very much as they did two and three decades ago. Even so, a reasonably modest increase in taxes, with the additional revenues targeted for families in poverty, could significantly reduce the extent of poverty without requiring the reduction of other federal expenditures. A shift in budget expenditures without a tax increase could accomplish the same result.

On the other hand, it may be argued that inadequacy lies not with the level of expenditures but with the structure and distribution of benefits. The appropriate budget allocation among the components of the welfare system depends primarily on the relative priorities of various goals and political constraints. As the discussion in Chapter 2 has indicated, cash is generally the most efficient income transfer form, offering the advantages of maximizing recipient choices while limiting administrative costs and interference with the market system. If command over goods in general is most important, consideration should be given to the cash-out of many of the existing in-kind transfer programs. Vouchers and other in-kind transfers also offer advantages when other social preferences are built into the welfare system. Both types attempt to direct or constrain the consumption of transferred income. Vouchers can be used to reduce the price and encourage the utilization of particular goods and services that are available in the market. Direct public provision of goods and services can be useful when special characteristics of a particular good or service make it inappropriate or impossible to be supplied through the private market mechanism at an equivalent cost, or when it is desirable to control the exact nature of the good or service provided. Thus as an alternative to a "cash strategy," consideration might be given to an in-kind approach whereby consumption needs in the areas of food, health, and housing would be assured, and supplemented by at most a modest cash transfer. These are two possible shifts in the distribution of the social transfer account. There are many alternative ways to allocate funds within a system. It should be recognized that to some extent different transfers can be interchangeable when there is a common goal, a fact that can be useful for compromising apparently conflicting goals and constraints in determining the distribution of the social transfer account.

Because of the interrelatedness of the major welfare programs, a holistic framework of analysis would seem useful. Conceptually, at least, the level and distribution of the transfer account should be jointly and simultaneously determined. In practice this would require coordination and cooperation between committees within the Congress and between departments within the executive. Alternatively, responsibility for all of the relevant transfer programs could be lodged in one committee and one agency or cabinet office. However the coordination is handled administratively, it is imperative that there be an effective overview authority.[86]

Program Characteristics

An understanding of the issues and techniques of integrating the welfare system is dependent on a comprehension of the general characteristics of welfare benefit structures and the difficulties caused by their interrelation. Discussions of these topics are included in the Appendix. However, the importance of the following characteristics are noted briefly in this chapter:

- Definition of filing unit—the group of persons which, in a legal and administrative sense, jointly applies for and receives benefits.

- Eligibility criteria—the method of restricting participation to the target group.

- Definition of countable income—the measure of income used to determine program eligibility and benefit entitlement.

- Benefit structure—the interdependent relationship of basic benefit level, marginal tax rate or benefit reduction rate, and breakeven point.

- Accounting period—the time period over which countable income is measured to determine eligibility and benefit payments.

The primary problem of interaction among welfare programs is that the characteristics of each welfare program are not coordinated with the other programs in the system. This has resulted in extensive duplication in administration, unintentional overlaps in benefit coverage, undesirable behavioral incentives for multiprogram participants, and numerous inequities.

Filing unit definitions and eligibility criteria serve the function of categorizing programs so that they benefit only a specific target population. This function necessitates some differences in criteria among programs. However, it is not evident that the actual range of variation is necessary. In fact the lack of uniformity of filing units and eligibility criteria in the system exists largely because program regulations have been developed independently and without consideration of the potential efficiency of eliminating unnecessary administrative overlap and duplication. The information needed to make eligibility and benefit determinations for all income-tested transfer programs is primarily the same, regardless of the specific criteria and calculation formulas. Efficiency could be increased greatly with uniform definitions and eligibility determination and, even where uniformity is not desirable, with administrative integration and cooperation.

Similarly, the definition of countable income is different in almost every program. Each has its own treatment of earned and unearned income and its own set of deductions and exemptions. As with variation in eligibility criteria, different treatments of income may be desirable in order to control recipient incentives. Again, however, much of the variation is unnecessary, and administrative integration could be facilitated by standardizing certain basic definitions, deductions, and exemptions.

Countable income definitions and the parameters that make up the benefit structures (that is, basic benefit level, tax rate, and breakeven point) also have a direct effect on recipient incentives. A multiprogram participant can find that benefits from different programs mount generously but that as this happens it becomes less advantageous to increase work effort—not necessarily because the welfare benefits provide a luxurious standard of living, but because a very large part of any increase in earnings is offset by reductions in multiprogram benefits. These problems resulting from high cumulative benefit reduction rates were discussed in Chapter 1. The complete interdependence of benefit levels, benefit reduction rates, and breakeven points makes the alleviation of the work incentive problem a difficult trade-off decision. Any action to lower benefit reduction rates requires that breakeven points be raised and/or benefit levels be lowered.

Program Integration

A systematic and calculated utilization of program integration techniques can eliminate some of the undesirable effects of an uncoordinated multiprogram welfare system. There are several tools that can be used to resolve conflicting program objectives and prevent excessive program overlap, as well as to effect specific behavioral incentives for program participants. The central feature of these tools is the use of countable income definitions and differential tax rates.

CASH-OUT

The concept of cash is perhaps the easiest method of integrating two programs. The idea behind it is to eliminate duplicative administration by replacing with cash the benefits of an in-kind program and merging the converted assistance with an existing cash transfer program. Such a proposed cash-out of the food stamp program was included in H.R. 1.

SEQUENCING

Sequencing uses the definition of countable income to link the benefit structures of two programs. Under this method the net benefits of one program are counted as income for purposes of eligibility and benefit determination for a second program. Thus the benefits of the first program are in effect taxed by the second program. This reduces the cost and coverage of the second and also reduces the combined benefit level of both programs together. AFDC benefits are currently counted as income for food stamps and public housing benefits. In general, cash assistance is counted as income for in-kind programs while the reverse is not true, primarily because of the difficulty of defining net benefits for in-kind programs.

FULL BENEFIT OFFSET

Full benefit offset reduces the benefit entitlement of one program by the total amount of net benefits received from another program, in effect taxing those benefits at the rate of 100 percent. This method can be used to eliminate overlapping coverage resulting from programs that are targeted at the same problem but for different population categories. It aims to compensate for holes in the classification process that impair horizontal equity. In the current system the amount of Social Security and Unemployment Insurance benefits are generally fully subtracted from AFDC benefits. This treatment may reflect a belief that these programs are intended to alleviate the same problem but for different population categories, and that recipients should not benefit from double coverage. The full benefit offset method can also be used to intentionally discourage simultaneous participation in certain welfare programs. In Chapter 6 it was pointed out that this full benefit offset leaves those who have contributed to Social Security no better off than welfare recipients who have not. The suggestion of taxing Social Security benefits at the earned income tax rate suggests a "partial benefit offset," defined just below.

PARTIAL BENEFIT OFFSET

This technique is used to tax benefits from other programs at a rate less than 100 percent. The partial benefit offset is a variation from the full benefit offset, and it can facilitate the imposition of various incentives for simultaneous participation in welfare programs. Congress has recently used this tool to prevent the total offset by various welfare programs of increases in Social Security benefits.

EXEMPTION

An exemption, also called a disregard or set-aside, is set by law and excludes a certain amount of income from welfare taxation by subtracting that amount from gross income. This tool can be used for equity and incentive purposes. It also has the effect of reducing the average welfare tax on gross income. The AFDC benefit determination includes a $30 monthly disregard. Other programs, like public housing, allow a specified exemption for each dependent as a living allowance.

EXPENSE DEDUCTION

The expense deduction is similar to the exemption in that it is subtracted from gross income before benefit determination. It is used to promote equity and to influence behavior. While the exemption is usually a standard amount, the expense deduction can vary according to demonstrable work or living expenses. It serves to reduce the burden (or the relative price, depending on the point of view) of certain types of necessary (or desirable) behavior. In essence, the government pays part of the cost of these expenses. In the food stamp program, for example, deductions from gross income before benefit determination include such things as child care payments, education fees, and medical expenses in excess of $10 per month.

EXPENSE REIMBURSEMENT

Sometimes called tax reimbursement, expense reimbursement is similar to and is often confused with expense deduction. While expense deduction is a partial subsidy dependent on the program tax rate, expense reimbursement is a total subsidy and is independent of the tax rate. In addition to the $30 monthly disregard, AFDC recipients get a reimbursement for allowable work-related expenses. (This is sometimes confusingly called an expense deduction, but the operation is clearly a reimbursement.) In addition, most states use this feature in AFDC benefit formulas to reimburse payroll and income taxes.

System Integration

The program integration methods discussed in the previous section are represented, if haphazardly, in the current welfare structure. The rationales for their uses have been primarily based on internal program considerations. It is now recognized that much of what is regarded as the "welfare mess" cannot be resolved only by internally restructuring individual welfare programs, and that in fact many of the problems exist because the proliferation of welfare programs has not been planned, evaluated, or even reformed as an interdependent system. A system orientation requires an *overall* strategy or structure that can be implemented to rationalize and coordinate all welfare programs in order to eliminate the haphazard incentive effects and reduce the administrative inefficiency associated with the current multiprogram welfare system. The system integration strategy alternatives outlined in this section use the program-linking tools (described in the previous section) in various ways with the common objective of dealing with cumulating benefits and excessively high welfare tax rates. The discussion that follows is brief and is intended only to provide a general introduction to the concepts involved. Because none of these proposed alternatives have ever been instituted, no real life examples can be given.

INDEPENDENT ADDITION

Independent addition is really a straw man and represents the absence of any rigorous system integration scheme. Income definitions used by each program exclude the benefits paid by all other programs and include only earned and other nontransfer income. Consequently, both the benefit levels and the benefit reduction rates cumulate additively for the multiprogram participant. This method is relatively generous to those whose earnings fall involuntarily, but is also generous to those who voluntarily reduce work effort, which may be tempting when effective benefit reduction rates can easily approach and exceed 100 percent. Under these circumstances a person may increase work effort and earned income only to experience a decrease in disposable income.[87]

An independent addition scheme tends to support high benefit levels and low breakeven points, but with the accompanying high cumulative tax rates that are destructive to economic work incentives.

CASH-OUT

Cash-out generally is a term used to describe the replacement of in-kind benefits with cash benefits. In the context of the integration of a welfare system, the various "cash-out" proposals entail the elimination of all current welfare programs—cash, voucher, goods and services—and the institution of a single NIT or refundable tax credit type cash assistance program. Most analysts agree that this approach would facilitate the control of cost, coverage, and the incentive effects, while eliminating the myriad administrative problems implicit in a multiprogram system. On the other hand, the desirability of cash-out must be judged according to the trade-offs between cash and in-kind assistance discussed in Chapter 2. Alternatively, selective cash-out has been proposed for one or more of the existing in-kind transfer programs, thereby simplifying and streamlining the welfare system without the political risks of the total cash-out approach. In general, a reduction in the number of welfare programs could possibly help to alleviate the cumulative tax rate problem, and would certainly facilitate program coordination and administrative integration.

ADMINISTRATIVE INTEGRATION

Administrative integration is a technique that can be used to merge the desired features of cash and in-kind transfers while, as in the previous alternative, the whole system is integrated into one program. Although, like the cash-out scheme, there is only one program and one benefit determination, the distinguishing feature of this proposal is that only part of that benefit is paid in cash, while the rest is paid in various vouchers—food and housing, for example. In this way some of the concerns of cash-out opponents are alleviated (an attempt is made to direct the expenditures of the recipient) while substantial cost savings could be realized through the elimination of multiple administration.

PROGRAM OFFSET

Program offset can be designed as a more politically palatable alternative to total cash-out. This approach compromises the single program and multiprogram systems. The full benefit offset technique is the basic feature, and is used so that while an eligible participant may receive benefits from more than one program, he is as well-off receiving benefits from one program (cash assistance) as he is from participating in *all* programs in the system. Thus there is no incentive for multiprogram participation. This has the advantage of allowing the coexistence of noncash programs for those who might be ineligible for cash assistance and for those who for some reason prefer in-kind benefits. This plan could also be useful as a transition to an all cash system.

TAX CEILING

This integration scheme is aimed directly at the problem of high cumulative marginal tax rates. With the tax ceiling approach the cash assistance program would guarantee that the total system marginal tax rate on additional earnings does not exceed some specified maximum that would be equal to or greater than the internal cash assistance program tax rate. This is done by calculating cash benefits after the benefits of all other programs have been calculated, and altering the internal tax rate, when necessary, to assure that the cumulative rate does not exceed the statutory maximum. All other programs can operate independently. It should be noted that once a person is enrolled in a package of programs that activate the tax ceiling, participation in additional programs becomes "free" since the cumulative tax rate cannot be increased. This could create horizontal inequities and undesirable incentives for multiprogram participation. The tax ceiling scheme does require some complex calculation procedures that might create or exacerbate administrative problems in all programs. In addition, this plan could necessitate time lags and overlapping accounting periods. Like any technique that would maintain basic benefit levels while reducing tax rates, the tax ceiling approach would raise the breakeven point, and thus would increase cost and coverage, which as always, is the price of fostering a more desirable work incentive structure.

VARIABLE TAX RATE

A variable tax rate schedule for the cash assistance program can attain the same advantages of the tax ceiling scheme, yet without the major administrative disadvantages. Under the tax ceiling plan, the cash assistance tax rate varies in response to changes in the *benefits* of other programs in order to impose a maximum tax rate. Under the alternative variable tax rate scheme the cash tax rate is dependent solely on *participation* in other programs. Thus tax rates can be controlled (and even effectively kept under a tax ceiling) without necessitating time lags, overlapping accounting periods, and other administrative complexities. In addition, the variable tax rate schedule can be structured to reduce the undesirable incentives for multiprogram participation that are implicit in the tax ceiling plan.

SEQUENCING

Sequencing every program within the system is another means of containing cumulative marginal tax rates. A structured ordering of programs is established so that countable income for any one program includes nontransfer income plus net transfer benefits from all programs that precede it in the established order. The effective marginal tax rate at any earnings level depends on the individual program tax rates, but can exceed neither the sum of those tax rates nor 100 percent. The primary advantage of sequencing as a system integration scheme is the mathematical prohibition of a cumulative marginal tax rate greater than 100 percent. While this is desirable, it cannot in itself guarantee a reasonable positive work incentive. It has the disadvantage of requiring very complex administrative procedures in a system with more than a few programs.

Conclusions

The last attempt at welfare reform centered on some very important horizontal equity considerations, primarily in its concern for the working poor. However, since it was to be a supplement to the rest of the welfare system, which would have remained largely unaltered, the Family Assistance Plan dealt inadequately with problems generated by the existence of a multiplicity of loosely coordinated programs with overlapping target populations, and would have left unsolved–in fact would have exacerbated–the equally important problem of vertical equity, and specifically the problem of high cumulative benefit reduction rates.

Any proposals for reform or replacement of the welfare system that arise out of this effort must not repeat this error. It must be understood that tax rates and income definitions are not just program characteristics of relatively little importance, but that they interact so as to dramatically affect behavioral incentives, and thus can be useful tools of welfare reform. The translation of that recognition into a rational and comprehensive systematic integration of programs is essential to the successful achievement of the primary objectives of an income-tested transfer system.

Summary and Conclusion

This paper is intended to serve three principal purposes: (1) to describe the current American welfare system, particularly its shortcomings; (2) to examine a wide variety of potential reform measures and the trade-off among various goals inherent in each (these measures range from proposals that would replace much of the present system to techniques for dealing with a host of individual problems); and (3) to lay out some of the basic questions that require resolution before substantial development of a specific reform approach is undertaken. *It is not intended to present specific alternatives for decision, but to provide a basic background for debate on welfare reform.*

The welfare system is one part of a two-part public transfer system comprised of (1) income-tested, cash and in-kind transfer programs such as AFDC, SSI, food stamps, Medicaid, and public housing; and (2) social insurance programs, such as Social Security, Unemployment Insurance, and Workmen's Compensation. This paper concentrates on the former set of programs, that is, on "welfare." However, the interface of the two cannot be ignored since they have similar functions and overlapping target populations.

Problems

It is generally agreed that the transfer system, and particularly its welfare component, is plagued by a number of severe shortcomings. Although it provides substantial income supplementation to many who need it, it nevertheless fails to some extent both those whom it is supposed to help and those who pay taxes. The "how" and "why" of this failure are, of course, not unrelated.

HOW THE SYSTEM HAS FAILED

- Across the country about 11 percent of the population remains poor (with an aggregate "poverty income gap" of about $12 billion).[88]

- In some states benefits are not sufficient to provide a minimally adequate standard of living while in others adequacy is achieved, at least for AFDC recipients, and in still other states or localities a combination of programs yields substantially more than a minimal standard of living for certain categories of recipients.

- In order to meet target efficiency goals, coverage has been made categorical and thus varies considerably across demographic groups. Twenty percent of those who are poor receive no public transfer payments at all. Ninety-seven percent of the aged who are poor before transfers receive benefits from one or another program, while only 51 percent of families with children headed by an ablebodied male who are poor before transfers receives any benefits.

- In general AFDC is a program for female-headed families, and thus many intact, male-headed families of the same size and income receive no benefits. This "horizontal inequity" can have the unintended result of inducing husbands to leave their families. Even in those states with an AFDC-Unemployed Fathers (UF) program, male family-heads must meet standards not required of female family-heads.

- Individual programs, as well as the system as a whole, contain work disincentives created by benefit reduction (or marginal tax) rates that approach and even exceed 100 percent, and by notches, which cause a precipitous loss in benefits when income rises above some breakeven point.

- The "system" is characterized by administrative overlap and inefficiency: taxpayers do not get a full return for their dollar and recipients must negotiate a bewildering array of programs when seeking help.

- The administrative inefficiency increases program cost in two ways. First, administrative costs themselves are unnecessarily high. Second, an inefficient system is subject to a higher incidence of error and abuse. The result is unnecessarily higher program costs.

WHY THE SYSTEM HAS FAILED

Surely no one intended such a system. But in the various efforts to provide for one or another specific need or group, little or no attention was paid to how a new program or a program change would interact with programs already in place. This is certainly one reason for the present poorly related set of programs.

But there is another, perhaps more fundamental, reason why it has failed. Many of the problems that exist in individual programs and that are exacerbated by the multiprogram nature of the system are there, at least implicitly, by design. While there is general agreement on a list of system goals, these goals are, by their nature, somewhat inconsistent. Thus, what is now viewed as a problem, or a damning program or system feature, happened to some extent as the inevitable result of coming down on one side or another of an unpleasant but necessary trade-off. The decision having been made, it is perhaps easier to criticize the result without considering the costs of the alternatives.

For example, most people seem to want benefits targeted on those most in need. They also seem to want to make certain that if a person's earnings increase, his take-home pay increases, and that his take-home pay is greater than that of another whose earnings did not rise. The latter goals can be assured by benefit reduction rates less than 100 percent, but such "marginal tax rates" imply transfers to those higher in the income distribution than otherwise might be desirable. Thus the goals of target efficiency, positive work incentive, and vertical equity are not mutually consistent. Marginal tax rates or breakeven points that are too high may be partly the result of technical problems with technical solutions, but unfortunately, they are also the result of basic policy choices. These choices will be considered again at the conclusion of this discussion.

It should be noted here that one policy that clearly suggests itself is a reduction in the number of executive branch agencies and Congressional committees dealing with welfare programs, and a better integration of those institutions exercising an oversight function for most of the complex transfer system.

Potential Reforms

In considering in this paper potential reform or replacement of the income-tested transfer system, the following have been used as general goals, recognizing that they are to some extent conflicting and must be compromised.[89] The order does not imply a ranking.

Adequacy. Although adequacy is both hard to agree upon and hard to measure, it still seems useful to design a welfare system in which those who work and those who cannot work have access to some level of income that is adequate for subsistence.

Horizontal Equity. People in similar circumstances should be treated similarly.

Vertical Equity. Those who earn more should take home more; those who need more should receive relatively more.

Work Incentives. Those who can work should find it strongly in their interest to do so.

Family Stability Incentives. Disincentives to family formation or incentives for family dissolution should be minimized.

Administrative Efficiency. The system should be as simple and straightforward as possible; administrative costs, burden on participants, and fraud and error should be minimized; system objectives should be fulfilled at minimum cost.

Target Efficiency. Benefits should be accurately targeted on those most in need and delivered in the most efficient form (cash, in-kind, or vouchers).

Independence. The system should be structured in a way that aids and encourages those who are able to become self-sufficient so that they will no longer require assistance. While often considered a goal of the welfare system, it is difficult to translate independence for the recipients into operational terms.

Coherency and Control. The system as a whole should be understandable in its operation and effects, have the intended effects, and be subject to policy and fiscal control.

Benefits can be transferred in three basic forms: cash, as in the AFDC program; vouchers, as in the food stamp program; or goods and services, as in public housing programs.

There is no reason why the three cannot be used simultaneously, if that best fulfills policy goals. Generally, cash is the most efficient transfer device and maximizes the options of the recipient. Vouchers can be used to effect a national policy of more equal access to a particular good or service while leaving to the individual the consumption decision within this category of goods or services. Direct provision of goods or services controls consumption more directly: this approach is useful when the supply of the good or service in question is not responsive to market demand, and the government thus has an interest and a responsibility for maintaining efficiently functioning markets.

If cash is selected as the principal transfer mechanism, a number of program structures are possible. As described in Chapter 2, refundable tax credits and negative income tax plans can be used efficiently to implement universal cash transfers. The former is fully integrated with the positive income tax structure while the latter is only partially so. Both have the potential to replace the present welfare system with a different structure and concept. If a categorical cash transfer program, like FAP or AFDC, is desired, a separate administrative apparatus would be required. Generally, as eligibility is more narrowly restricted to certain categories of poor persons, the administrative complexities become greater.

It is also possible to mix cash and in-kind transfers. Such a course might commend itself if the desire to control consumption uses of transfer dollars is compelling and/or if the popularity of in-kind transfers (whether by voucher or commodity) would make possible a more adequate total package. If some sort of housing voucher is proposed as a result of the Department of Housing and Urban Development's (HUD) review of the present set of housing programs, an opportunity and a challenge would be presented. The desire to build regional cost of living differentials into the welfare system could then be effected by providing a uniform federal cash benefit while continuing to base housing transfers on local costs. Since the target population for the cash transfer and the housing voucher would overlap (the degree of overlap itself being a policy decision), the programs would have to be carefully integrated.

The adoption of a mix of cash and in-kind programs precludes a simple administrative structure. Such a course also requires that much attention be given to the relationships between a variety of income-tested programs, targeted at the same population. Care should be taken that neither basic benefits nor benefit reduction rates cumulate to undesirably high levels. As noted, strong political pressures surround noncash transfer programs, making them difficult to alter or cash out. Finally, as Chapter 2 shows, moving from a simple universal cash transfer to a mixed cash-in-kind system with a work requirement introduces administrative complexities and inequities. That is, program structures become more complex and the degree to which the primary policy goals can be fulfilled successfully is reduced when the system is asked to address many concerns simultaneously.

In addition to a decision in favor of categorical coverage, it may also be desirable to condition benefits for certain classes of recipients on employment or training for employment. A range of work-conditioned transfers and mixed work-nonwork programs (such as FAP-OFP) are then possible. Chapter 4 examines a wide range of such programs, pointing out their pros and cons relative to the cash programs discussed above. Generally, they have theoretical advantages in terms of monetary incentives to work, and they do tie benefits to work effort. However, one must ask if the additional benefits are worth the additional costs. The additional costs occur because of (1) the problems that follow yet another categorization of the population and (2) the considerable dollar costs and administrative burdens of operating the programs.

On the basis of existing evidence that the work orientation of the poor does not differ substantially from that of the rest of society, it is not clear that it is necessary to incur the costs. The evidence is perhaps stronger that the wide range of manpower services provided for in the present AFDC-WIN structure has had very little effect in aiding the poor to increase their earnings. Indeed, the weight of the evidence seems to argue that if tying transfer benefits to work effort is to be a major policy goal, more reliance should be placed upon creation of jobs for welfare recipients and less on an elaborate set of work registration requirements.

Finally, whatever the degree of coverage and multiplicity of benefit types, there will be a need to provide for a much better integration of income-tested transfer programs (and these with social insurance programs) than is manifested in our present system. There are many technical tools available for accomplishing this, which are described in Chapter 7, but the choice of which ones to apply is inextricably bound up with important policy concerns. For example, consider the following:

- If housing voucher and cash programs are both covering the same population, decisions should be made regarding how benefits from one program are to be treated in determining payment levels in the other. How this is done has implications for the cumulative benefit level, the cumulative benefit reduction rate, and the relative magnitude of outlays under each program for a given total outlay.

- The idea of a common means test administered by one agency on behalf of some of the major welfare programs has considerable merit. However, for this to be feasible, many of the technical program characteristics discussed in the Appendix (definitions of filing unit and accounting period, for example) that can have a major impact on costs and coverage should be consistent.

Broad Policy Questions

The previous discussion has raised a number of issues, the resolution of which will essentially shape public policy on transfers to the low-income population and substantially influence the structure of particular welfare programs. To focus the discussion, these issues may be summarized as follows:[90]

> *Who* is to receive benefits?
>
> *How* are the transfers to be effected: cash vs. voucher vs. goods and services; degree of work-relatedness; technical program structure?
>
> *How much* is to be transferred; that is, what are the benefit levels to be?

The first question raises the issue of coverage. The options range from having one universal cash program that is integrated with the tax system and results in the elimination of the welfare system to having a multicategory, multitype benefit structure not dissimilar to that now in place. Many feasible possibilities lie in between. Trying to do better with respect to transfer system goals (adequacy, equity, work and family stability incentives, and administrative and target efficiency) raises the possibility of broader coverage of certain groups in a reformed or replacement system as well as greater program consolidation and integration. But broad coverage involves a host of other issues, such as program structure, work requirements, and the like. Because of its implications for cost and caseloads, as well as for human welfare, the coverage decision is perhaps the most important of all those that will have to be made.

The second question, the "how" question, unmasks a set of issues that will determine program structure. Earlier some of the issues surrounding the form of the benefit were noted briefly. The three forms can co-exist, as is the case with the present welfare system. However, they must be properly integrated.

How work-conditioned should benefits be? Obviously, this depends to some extent on whether or not intact families are covered. But there is considerable pressure already to require female family-heads with young children to work. As part of the decision-making process here, the following issues must be examined: the scale of day care provision, the efficacy of manpower services, the meaning of "employability," the best way to provide work incentives, and the price that society is willing to pay to effect and enforce work requirements. Implied also is a basic decision on the relative priority to be given to four methods of "conditioning" transfers to supposedly employable adults to meet public concern: work opportunities (public employment), work incentives (low benefit reduction rates), work registration (as in the present WIN program), and a work-related benefit (as in a program that ties the benefit to remuneration from work, like an earnings supplement).

Technical questions of program structure, such as the accounting period, used to be relegated to a lower order of importance, but no longer is this possible. Experience over the past few years has shown the tremendous impact on costs, numbers of recipients, equity, and efficiency that follow from technical program features. Moreover, the failure to explicitly account for the interaction of a wide range of cash and in-kind income-tested transfers has resulted in an inequitable and inefficient system, as demonstrated by the recent concern over cumulative benefit reduction rates. Thus policymakers must also consider technical questions previously examined only at lower levels.

The third question addresses adequacy, incentives, and the distribution of income. To perhaps oversimplify, the issues may be summarized by recalling the inexorable arithmetic of basic benefits, benefit reduction (marginal tax) rates, and breakevens that characterize any income-tested program. The basic benefit determines the degree of adequacy for those with no other income. Along with the tax rate, the basic benefit determines the level of the breakeven income and thus coverage and work incentives. These program characteristics determine how much will be transferred and at what cost. Here, too, a number of related issues will be settled. The antipoverty effect of a new program clearly depends on what level of benefits is ultimately determined to be "adequate." Furthermore, the political acceptability of any program will depend greatly on benefit levels and total cost.

Each of the questions examined above is but the skeleton of an issue. However, each cuts away many side issues and forces a decision. *It is vitally important to recognize that these decisions are highly interdependent.* Indeed, this interdependence is a theme that runs throughout the text to emphasize that each major area for policy decision cannot be considered in a vacuum. It must be clearly understood that the root of many of the problems with the present system was the desire, expressed in policy decisions made over a period of time, to provide assistance only to some of the needy and to provide that aid in various forms. In order to avoid a re-creation of the present system, the interdependency of the policy decisions must be recognized and acted upon. The first step is a weighing of concerns in the areas suggested by each of the above questions.

Appendix

Technical Characteristics of Income-Tested Transfer Programs

The primary characteristics of all income-tested transfer programs (SSI, AFDC, food stamps, and NIT) include the following: definition of the filing unit; eligibility criteria; definition of countable income; benefit schedule (basic benefit level, benefit reduction rate, and breakeven level); and accounting period. A major program interrelation problem is to make these characteristics compatible across programs in a way that maximizes the target efficiency of the transfers, minimizes administrative burdens, minimizes error and fraud, minimizes adverse behavioral incentives, and fosters vertical and horizontal equity. Due to the nature of transfer programs, some of these conflicting goals may have to be compromised. Each of these characteristics will be examined briefly.

Filing Unit. The filing unit is that group of persons that, in a legal and administrative sense, jointly applies for and receives benefits. In the food stamp program, the filing unit is a broadly defined group called a household, which may include unrelated persons. The AFDC program, on the other hand, employs narrower definitions that frequently divide an extended family living together into more than one unit. Both definitions of filing unit make sense within the context of their respective programs. If these or similar programs are to be better coordinated or combined, however, difficult choices on the appropriate filing unit will have to be made.

Eligibility Criteria. In an income-tested transfer program there is by definition, at least the criterion of income level, usually in relation to family size. Depending on the program, there may be additional eligibility criteria based on factors such as asset levels, family composition, residence, employability, and willingness to work. Sometimes eligibility for one program depends upon participation in another (Medicaid in some locations, for example). Among the problems relating to eligibility criteria are these:

- Eligibility criteria do not always relate directly to need and may set up socially undesirable incentives (family break-up and migration, for example).

- Eligibility criteria are not uniform across programs even when the programs are intended to have similar target populations.

- Many low-income households are eligible for several programs yet the administration of these programs is not well coordinated. This can lead to great disparities in benefit levels with a small number of fortunate recipients receiving relatively generous total benefits. Furthermore, the tax rates of each program can add up to very high total marginal tax rates (see below). The solution is not to forbid recipients from receiving benefits from more than one program, but to better coordinate administration, including perhaps a reduction in the number of such programs.

Countable Income. Countable income is that measure of income used to determine benefits. Changes in countable income also occasion changes in benefits; thus it is this income concept that is relevant in examining marginal tax rates. Countable income definitions vary from program to program. For example, in determining income for the purposes of computing food stamp program benefits, AFDC benefits are counted, but the reverse is not true, since it would be nearly impossible to uniquely calculate benefit levels if each one were dependent on the level of the other. What is essential is that the interdependence of income definitions be recognized so that they can be rationally coordinated to avoid undesirable interactions.

Benefit Schedule. A program's benefit structure defines the amount of benefits at various levels of income; in other words, it defines the relationship between countable income and disposable income for all eligible households. This relationship can most easily be defined in terms of three measures (which may not be equal for all eligible families, in which case one can think of a series of benefit schedules).

The *basic benefit level* is the benefit an eligible unit would receive if the unit had no countable income during the period in question. In other words, it is the disposable income the unit would have if its countable income were zero. This level should be high enough to assure a minimally adequate standard of living.

The *marginal tax rate* is the percentage of additional earnings that are "taxed away" through a decrease in the transfer payment. This might be more accurately called the *benefit reduction rate.* It is desirable to keep this rate well below 100 percent in order to reward those who work, both out of a sense of fairness and to preserve the recipient's economic incentive to work. In most schemes, this implicit tax rate is uniform, but proposals have been made that vary the tax rate according to level or source of income.

The third characteristic of a benefit schedule is the *breakeven level of income.* This is the income at which a person no longer receives any benefits from the program. The higher the breakeven level, the more persons will be receiving benefits under the program and consequently the higher the program costs.

The basic dilemma in designing an income transfer system is that these three characteristics are not independent. Once two of these are set, the third is automatically determined. For example, if the guarantee is set at $3,000 and the marginal tax rate at 100 percent, then the breakeven level is $3,000. If the guarantee is set at $4,000 and the marginal tax rate is 33 percent, the breakeven level is $12,000. In the simple case of a uniform marginal tax rate, the relationship can be represented by this formulation.[91]

$$\text{Breakeven} = \frac{\text{basic benefit level}}{\text{marginal tax rate}}$$

Thus it is impossible to set a high benefit level and a low tax rate without causing a high breakeven level and, hence, a high program cost. When recipients are eligible for more than one program, the basic benefit level (that is, the sum of all basic benefit levels) is raised but so, too, is the total marginal tax rate arising from the multiple reductions in benefits as countable income rises. Various integration schemes, discussed in Chapter 7, have been proposed to deal with this problem of cumulative tax rates. As the above makes clear, however, this can only be done by either lowering the cumulative basic benefit level or increasing the breakeven level. There is no easy solution. Technical adjustments will not enable the avoidance of allocation decisions.

Accounting Period. The accounting period is the time period over which countable income is measured to determine eligibility and payment levels.[92] Transfer program benefits are generally distributed monthly, but incomes of the low-income population tend to fluctuate a good deal from month to month. Also, program structures are often defined in terms of annual income. It would be desirable to have an accounting system for transfer programs that ensures that a family with a temporarily low monthly income does not receive benefits at the expense of permanently low income families and that changes in family income and status are promptly fed into the benefit computation process. Such an accounting system would be complex enough from the point of view of one program, let alone two or more. Nevertheless, such a system is, if anything, more important in a multiprogram world. For obvious reasons, it is important for program A to know what needs program B is fulfilling at a point in time and over time.

Notes to Part One

1. President Richard M. Nixon, Welfare Reform Address, August 8, 1969.

2. U.S. Congress, Joint Economic Committee (JEC), Subcommittee on Fiscal Policy, *Studies in Public Welfare* (Washington, D.C.: U.S. Government Printing Office, 1972-74). See bibliography for separate paper listings. See also Irene Lurie, editor, *Integrating Income Maintenance Programs* (New York: Academic Press, forthcoming).

3. Excluded from this list are the property ownership and income system and the intrafamily transfer system.

4. The benefit reduction rate is the rate at which as earnings increase benefits are reduced. An additional dollar of earned income in AFDC, for example, reduces the benefit by 67 cents, leaving a net increase in total income of 33 cents. The effect is thus the same as if a marginal tax of 67 percent were applied to earnings. The two terms, benefit reduction rate and marginal tax rate, can be used interchangeably in this paper. The Appendix contains a fuller discussion of this and other basic characteristics of income-tested programs.

5. The poverty threshold concept is used throughout this paper as a proxy for some sort of more refined adequacy standard, primarily because the available data are often analyzed with reference to this concept. While this standard is often not fully appropriate to the topics of discussion in the paper, it should not do injustice to the conclusions drawn.

6. It has been estimated that overall about 78 percent of those eligible for AFDC participate in the AFDC program. Within the overall program, the percentages are 91 percent for female heads and 37 percent for AFDC-UF. See Barbara Boland, "Participation in the Aid to Families with Dependent Children Program," Urban Institute Working Paper 97102, June 19, 1973, Table 3, p. 20.

7. These jurisdictions include the 50 states, District of Columbia, Guam, Puerto Rico, and the Virgin Islands. No state is required to have a welfare program. As a condition of federal cost sharing, states are bound by the legal constraints of the Social Security Act and the regulations promulgated by DHEW under authority granted by the Act.

8. For the reasons cited, many states have abandoned the complex needs standard and have adopted one or another variant of a flat grant system. This trend can be expected to continue, particularly with the pressure of DHEW's Quality Control Sampling System. See footnote 29 for further information on this system.

9. While the law requires each participating jurisdiction to have a needs standard, it does not require that it actually pay that level of benefits.

10. See papers by Irene Lurie and Joseph Heffernan, in JEC, *Studies in Public Welfare,* Paper No. 5 (Part 2).

11. Food stamps are not available in those few counties which have chosen the food commodity distribution program. However, beginning July 1, 1974, all counties will be required to offer food stamps.

12. If recipients have become ineligible because of an increase in earnings, they retain Medicaid eligibility for 4 months.

13. After this paper was written the Administration introduced, in February 1974, a comprehensive health insurance proposal. It would provide universal entitlement to comprehensive health services coverage either through employer-based plans or as a government-assured plan. Costs would be subsidized for the low-income population under the government-assured plan with the level of subsidy reduced as the recipients' income rises.

14. The Housing Task Force in a report delivered in the fall of 1973 concluded that the primary reason people live in inadequate housing is that they have insufficient incomes, and that the current mix of housing programs has failed because this problem has not been addressed directly. Therefore, the Task Force recommended a shift from a supply-oriented strategy based on subsidies to producers and owners of housing to a demand-oriented strategy based on subsidies to consumers who have insufficient resources to buy or rent adequate housing. President Nixon, in his Housing Message of September 1973, supported the concept of housing allowances for the poor. Evaluative results from the current housing allowance experiments and further study of the relationship between a housing allowance and other welfare programs will form the foundation for any Administrative proposal in this area.

15. There is also a small ($35,251,000 in FY 1973) federally financed emergency assistance program.

16. The Michigan Survey Research Center (SRC) data were used in preference to figures published by the Bureau of the Census because the SRC data include the bonus value of food stamps in the definition of income and because they allow greater flexibility in presenting data for different family types. However, utilization of Census data would show patterns of coverage similar to the results presented here.

17. The term "families" as used here includes childless couples and unrelated individuals. The reader is warned that this definition consistently understates the relative importance of families with children in that each such "family" in poverty represents an average of nearly three individuals in poverty.

18. These calculations are based upon the Social Security Administration's poverty index for 1971. The poverty threshold in 1971 for a four-person urban family was then $4,113.

19. The General Accounting Office (GAO) survey was conducted at the request of the Subcommittee on Fiscal Policy of the Joint Economic Committee of Congress. Information was gathered from the records of 100 programs including public assistance, Social Security, veterans benefits, unemployment compensation, and many programs offering aid in the form of food, health care, housing, child care, and other basic services.

20. See JEC, *Studies in Public Welfare,* Paper Nos. 1 and 6.

21. The SSI program was not in existence and the recent Social Security increases were not in effect when the data were collected. Starting in 1974, the percentage of posttransfer poverty will be somewhat lower for the aged, blind, and disabled.

22. See footnote 16.

23. See footnote 19.

24. This example and numerous others can be found in JEC, *Studies in Public Welfare,* Paper No. 8.

25. A cumulative marginal tax rate defines the change in total net transfer payments per dollar change in earnings.

26. The subject of cash versus in-kind transfers is taken up again later in the paper when an attempt is made to establish some criteria for the selection of the most efficient form of transfer under selected conditions.

27. JEC, *Studies in Public Welfare,* Paper No. 5 (Part 1).

28. Eligibility criteria and income definitions of AFDC programs differ from state to state, however.

29. The Quality Control System was instituted to determine the extent to which eligibility determinations and benefit calculations are incorrect and to minimize the incidence of both eligibility and payment errors. The program requires that each state periodically select a statewide statistical sample of all cases and analyze the sample findings to determine the incidence of errors. Where tolerance levels are exceeded, plans for bringing error rates down to acceptable levels must be implemented. States with error rates over the allowable limits will be subject to reduced federal matching for public assistance. The tolerance levels that have been established for states to meet by July 1, 1975, are 3 percent error on eligibility and 5 percent on overpayments. (Data available after this paper was finished show that in the April to September 1973 period, sample findings revealed a nationwide error rate of 10.2 percent on eligibility, 22.8 percent on overpayments, and 8.1 percent on underpayments.)

30. See *Summary Report: New Jersey Graduated Work Incentive Experiment,* U.S. Department of Health, Education, and Welfare (December 1973).

31. The term "families" is used in the broad sense that includes unrelated individuals as one-person families.

32. See James N. Morgan et al., *Five Thousand American Families–Patterns of Economic Progress,* Vols. 1 and 2 (University of Michigan: Institute for Social Research, 1974).

33. Note that this definition of "at risk" includes persons who were below their poverty threshold for the entire period.

34. U.S. National Center for Social Statistics, *Findings of the 1971 AFDC Study,* Social Rehabilitation Service, U.S. Department of Health, Education, and Welfare (Washington, D.C.: U.S. Government Printing Office, 1972).

35. Shelter is a marginal example. In many geographical areas, if a family is to be able to afford safe and sanitary housing, it may require an income well above the poverty level. It is unlikely that the political process would tolerate the provision of a basic benefit level of cash assistance significantly higher than the poverty standard, even to the least controversial categories of welfare recipients, so that they could afford adequate housing.

36. The analysis of individual programs, which is necessary to fully support the conclusions of this argument, is beyond the scope of this paper. A few of the possibilities that have been suggested are cashing-out food stamps, providing vouchers for institutional manpower training, and eliminating certain social services in favor of cash.

37. The figure of $4,000 for an urban family of four is just a benchmark. Different size families in different living situations would obviously have different requirements. For example, the equivalent figure for a rural family with only two members might be as low as $1,600. This figure is also intended to reflect both federal and state shares under whatever financial relationships might exist. Seen in this light, $4,000 for an urban family of four may be a realistic minimum that one could expect to have to provide if such things as food stamps, and housing programs, were to be cashed out. However, it should be kept in mind that if coverage were provided to all families, only a very small proportion would actually receive the full amount of the basic benefit. The vast majority would have income from other sources and would be receiving small amounts of transfers.

38. Substantial work disincentives and incentives for undesirable (or disincentives for desirable) changes in family structure are the most relevant here.

39. For a detailed discussion of the administrative issues associated with various welfare reform plans see David N. Kershaw and Barbara Levitz Lindheim, *Administrative Issues in Planning and Implementing Welfare Reform Proposals* (Princeton, N.J.: Mathematica, Inc., 1973).

40. The low-income allowance does not rise with the cost of living, while poverty thresholds do, since the latter are stated in real income terms

and the former in fixed dollar terms. Thus, some families in poverty will be paying taxes in 1973.

41. The issue of work disincentives can only be settled by empirical evidence. This is the subject of a lengthy discussion in Chapter 3.

42. See the Appendix for a fuller explanation of "basic benefit" and "breakevens."

43. Many tax reform economists are advocating a broadened tax base with a constant benefit reduction rate for all income levels above poverty (after personal exemptions). These ideas fit well with a refundable tax credit. A constant tax rate would greatly simplify the administration of a credit. Evidence indicates that our present rate is only nominally progressive and, in fact, roughly proportional in its incidence due to tax avoidance among the well-to-do sanctioned by a complicated definition of taxable income. Thus, a switch to a constant tax rate and a more comprehensive definition of taxable income would not change substantially the relative tax burden among income classes, and would eliminate wasteful expenditures on tax avoidance. Further, a constant tax rate makes possible the calculation and disbursement of a family's net tax or transfer on a regular (say, monthly) basis. Frequent disbursements are important to those in poverty, who are by definition without the resources to meet their immediate needs. Finally, with a constant tax rate on all sources of income, variations in the periodic amount or source of income cannot lead to end-of-year, over- or under-payment of taxes. Therefore, there would be no end-of-year settling up, which is particularly troublesome for a low-income family that has received too much in transfers and has to find the resources to pay the excess back in one large sum.

44. Both of these objections would be ameliorated, although not entirely eliminated, if the NIT were to be administered by the Internal Revenue Service even though not fully integrated with the positive tax system in the way that a refundable tax credit would be. This might require some minor modifications in the existing administrative structure of the positive tax system. However, if all individuals and families report their incomes to one agency, no distinctions between the poor and nonpoor need be made. Audit procedures such as those now used to verify the accuracy of income tax reports would be utilized to determine the accuracy of the reports of income transfer recipients.

45. The Mega proposal approach to welfare reform put forth by Elliot Richardson in the fall of 1972 offers a possible way of structuring strong work incentives into an NIT for all families while minimizing the administrative costs and complexities. This plan is discussed in detail in Chapter 5.

46. In fact, all of these considerations mentioned above led to FAP becoming such a Christmas tree that at one point only $.7 billion of the estimated $4.5 billion net additional federal outlays (including the cashing-out of food stamps) over current law in FY 1974 would have gone toward increased cash benefits to families, while $1.7 billion was earmarked for support services and another $.7 billion for administration and the remaining $1 billion for fiscal relief for the states.

47. The Talmadge Amendment to WIN required all employable AFDC applicants to register for training or employment as a condition of eligibility, required state welfare agencies to provide necessary social and supportive services to all such registrants, and required that no less than 1/3 of WIN appropriations be spent for on-the-job training and public service employment.

48. Note that the major noncash programs that fit this description—for example, food stamps and public housing—also have an NIT type of structure. It is, of course, the compounding of their basic benefit levels and benefit reduction rates with those of the cash assistance programs that leads to undesirably large work disincentives and benefit levels for many multiple program recipients. These problems and potential solutions are a topic of Chapter 7.

49. The technical term for this is the "income effect."

50. *Summary Report: New Jersey Graduated Work Incentive Experiment,* U.S. Department of Health, Education, and Welfare (December 1973). See also *Income Maintenance and Labor Supply,* Glen G. Cain and Harold W. Watts, eds. (Chicago: Rand McNally, 1973).

51. The technical term for this is the "substitution effect."

52. For a full discussion of the results see *Summary Report: New Jersey Graduated Work Incentive Experiment,* U.S. Department of Health, Education, and Welfare (December 1973).

53. David S. Franklin, "A Longitudinal Study for WIN Dropouts: Program and Policy Implications," University of Southern California, (April 1972).

54. Leonard Goodwin, *Do the Poor Really Want to Work?* (Washington, D.C.: The Brookings Institution, 1972).

55. A "disregard" sets a zero tax on earnings up to some level. Thus, in the current AFDC structure, the first $30 of monthly earnings are disregarded or not taxed.

56. The term "employable" has come to have a meaning in policy discourse that is not very closely related to the person or the labor market. Briefly, if someone or some class is referred to as "employable," it means that the person or class should work.

57. Some analysts have noted how low productivity was during the second World War, though this might also have been due to the pressures on production capacity.

58. The day care issue itself is quite complex. Such questions as center versus home care, staff to child ratios, training of day care personnel, fee schedules and disregards, and transportation requirements must all be settled. As it relates to employability, advocacy of day care remains a value judgment issue.

59. The version of FAP reported out of the House Ways and Means Committee in 1971 provided for a net increase in federal outlays of $1.7 billion for manpower and support services versus $.7 billion in increased federal outlays for benefits to families.

60. For a review of the literature see Jon Goldstein, "The Effectiveness of Manpower Training Programs: A Review of Research on the Impact on the Poor," in JEC *Studies in Public Welfare,* Paper No. 3.

61. The last clause of this sentence expresses a sentiment that is consistent with policy in this area but is not consistent with an emerging view of husband-wife responsibilities.

62. Eight hundred million dollars in the House-passed H.R. 1 and open-ended funding in the Senate Finance Committee versions were proposed for public service employment.

63. Frequently the avowed purpose of work relief is to discourage potentially employable, potential welfare recipients from applying for welfare. Transition to a better job is not a goal.

64. There would, of course, have to be some means of adjudicating disputes.

65. The earnings supplement is discussed in considerable detail in Robert Haveman, Irene Lurie, and Thad Mirer, "Earnings Supplementation Plans for 'Working Poor' Families: An Evaluation of Alternatives," Institute for Research on Poverty, Discussion Paper 175-73, Madison, Wisconsin.

66. H.R. 3153 (93d Congress, 1st Session) Title I, Part B, November 30, 1973.

67. See the British Green Paper, *Proposals for a Tax-Credit System,* Cmnd. 5116 (London: HMSO, 1972).

68. The tax rate is a constant 30 percent up to 100 pounds ($250) of weekly income. Above that level a higher tax rate would apply. However, this would affect only a small percentage of earners.

69. See footnote 45.

70. See Henry J. Aaron, *Why Is Welfare So Hard to Reform?* (Washington, D.C.: The Brookings Institution, 1973).

71. The earnings "ceiling" rose to $13,200 in January 1974.

72. See Edward R. Fried et al., *Setting National Priorities: The 1974 Budget* (Washington, D.C.: The Brookings Institution, 1973), pp. 57-63. This calculation is based on the assumption that the employer share is effectively paid by the employee. (With a higher ceiling of $13,200, this figure has been recalculated to $13,800.)

73. This figure is based on the employee share only.

74. This is not necessarily undesirable, since a random incidence of unemployment would in itself greatly reduce poverty among unemployables.

75. This program has been replaced by the Supplemental Security Income program (SSI).

76. This would involve major changes in the AFDC-UF program. Unemployment would no longer be a condition of eligibility, the 100-hour-per-month limitation would be removed, UI eligibility would no longer preclude AFDC-UF eligibility, and the requirement of previous attachment to the labor force would be dropped.

77. While these programs are treated as a group here, the discussion in Chapter 4 of their relative strengths and weaknesses should be recalled.

78. This takes into consideration benefits provided by other programs, such as food stamps.

79. Keep in mind FAP cashed out food stamps so that the opportunities for multiple program participation would have been somewhat reduced. It is assumed here that any major reform would consider other programs so that total benefits would be distributed more evenly.

80. The term "hold harmless" indicates a provision in the legislation that states would not be required to supplement a basic national benefit beyond some earlier state expenditure level.

81. The specific income level depends on the level of AFDC benefits and the size of the earnings subsidy.

82. A notice of proposed rule-making to standardize the definition of incapacity was published by DHEW in February 1974.

83. That is, Medicaid benefits are fully retained as long as a person is eligible for AFDC. If income rises above the AFDC breakeven, Medicaid eligibility is terminated in four months.

84. The poverty threshold for an urban family of four was $4,275, only 38 percent of the $11,116 median family income.

85. Unfortunately, there are no historical data that include the value of income transferred in-kind.

86. A problem with the holistic view of the transfer system could present itself if the present range of programs, in fact, masks the true overall redistributional effect and if that redistribution is basically unpopular. From the pure "give 'em something" point of view, the present set of arrangements maintains a constituency of sorts for a range of programs that transfers consumption resources to the poor. The reorganization that may be implicit in the holistic view might blunt the different constituencies, and they might neither merge nor reappear.

87. Our current system, though lacking an overall strategy for system-wide integration, does manage to mitigate some of the effects of independent addition. For example, the food stamp and housing programs, by treating cash benefits (such as AFDC) as countable income, prevent benefits and tax rates from cumulating additively.

88. Imputation of all noncash benefits and correction of income underreporting would act to reduce these figures, although the fact that the Census and Current Population Survey undercount the number of poor persons would act in the opposite direction.

89. This list is not meant to be exhaustive. Other goals frequently mentioned are the contribution of the system to economic stability, a degree of flexibility necessary to adjust benefits to the changing status of recipients and the economic situation, and the minimization of unnecessary discretionary authority vested in program administrators.

90. The question of federal-state relations or what level of government will administer which parts of the transfer system is, in terms of importance, on an equal footing with the questions that follow. However, it is thought to be of a different dimension than the questions examined here. Needless to

say, policy-making in this area must consider federal-state relations once basic decisions on program structure are made.

91. If there is an initial 100 percent disregard before increases in countable income cause a reduction in benefits, the relationship is:

$$\text{Breakeven} = \frac{\text{basic benefit level}}{\text{marginal tax rate}} + \text{disregard}$$

92. One could distinguish between the "accounting period" or the time period over which income is measured to determine current benefits and the "accountable period" or the time period over which income is measured to determine the total entitlement for the period so as to preserve long-run equity among families.

Glossary

Average tax rate. Net taxes paid to the government as a percentage of income. Tax rates are called "nominal" if net income is used as the base and "effective" if gross or total income is used. In a welfare program, it is the total benefit reduction as a percentage of income.

Basic benefit level. The benefit received when the recipient has no income or, in AFDC, no countable income.

Breakeven level. In a welfare program, the level of earnings at which the recipient ceases to receive benefits from the government.

Cash out. Replacing an in-kind or voucher program with a roughly equivalent amount of cash benefits.

Categorical programs. Transfer programs in which eligibility is defined not only by income, but by additional factors, such as demographic characteristics (for example, age or number of parents present) or disability.

Countable income. In a welfare program, the income measure used to determine program eligibility and benefit level. It is determined by excluding certain items, such as irregular earnings or a child's earnings, from gross income. In AFDC, it specifically denotes the income measure applied against the basic benefit to determine the actual payment due. Countable income is used in its more general sense in this paper.

Cumulative tax rate. The total dollar reduction in benefits received from all transfer programs caused by a one dollar increase in recipient's earnings.

Disregard (set aside). If a transfer program has a zero benefit reduction rate until some level of earned income is reached, that level is the disregard or set aside. The disregard in the current AFDC program is $30 per month.

Horizontal equity. People in similar circumstances (for example, in similar need) should receive similar treatment.

In-kind benefits. Transfer benefits that come directly in the form of a good or service. Sometimes authors will use "in-kind" to include voucher payments in which case "in-kind" means the same as noncash.

Intact family. A family with two parents present. Most, but not all, male-headed families will be intact. As used in the paper, all working poor families are intact, but they are a subset of the total intact family population.

Marginal tax rate (benefit reduction rate). The dollar reduction in benefits that occurs when a recipient's earned income increases by one dollar.

Need standard. The income level, set by each state, that is used to determine eligibility for AFDC. Many states do not pay the full need standard as the basic benefit level.

Notch. An extreme case of high benefit reduction (usually over a very small range) where a very small increase in earnings will cause a very large drop in benefits (for example, moving over the AFDC income ceiling and thereby losing all Medicaid benefits).

Social insurance. Transfers based in part on previous contributions of the worker and/or his employer (for example, Social Security and unemployment compensation).

Target efficiency. The extent to which benefits go to those who need them.

Transfers. Benefits received from the government not in payment for goods or services.

Vertical equity. Those in relatively greater need should receive relatively larger benefits; those who earn more should have relatively larger disposable incomes.

Vouchers. Another form of noncash benefits. Instead of receiving the good or service directly, vouchers are purchasing power that is restricted to a particular category of goods or services (food stamps, for example).

Welfare. Transfers where the benefits are based on the recipient's income. Welfare programs are sometimes referred to as "means-tested" or "income-tested" programs.

Part Two

Toward an Effective Income Support System: An Overview Paper

Irwin Garfinkel

The author is deeply indebted to Felicity Skidmore for major editorial assistance; to D. Lee Bawden, Glen Cain, Robert Lampman, and particularly, Robert Haveman from the Poverty Institute for many helpful comments and suggestions; and to the conference participants for providing most of the arguments made in this essay.

Toward an Effective Income Support System: An Overview Paper

On March 11, 1974, a conference sponsored by the Institute for Research on Poverty was held to discuss the HEW Task Force paper and the paper's implications for the nation's income-tested transfer system. In the course of that conference, the strengths and shortcomings of the HEW analysis were appraised as were some of the policy strategies implicit in the document. This essay is designed to summarize many of the issues discussed at the conference and, in addition, to raise other related issues that must be considered in designing policies to alter the nation's income transfer system.

Central to the debate on this question is the issue of whether a complete overhaul of existing programs is more desirable than an extension and improvement of the current system. Should the whole patchwork of existing programs be replaced with one or at most two new universal programs as the arguments in the HEW paper suggest, or is it preferable to retain the existing programs, reform the structure of AFDC, AFDC-UF, and UI, and add certain new programs—such as a work bonus and/or a housing allowance?[1]

The proponents of an incremental approach stress that substantial progress has been made in reforming the nation's income transfer system in the last ten years. They point out that while the justifications being given now for a radical change are the same ones advanced ten years ago, impressive changes have already occurred. The expansion of the food stamp program and the liberalization of AFDC; the introduction of Medicare (which provides medical care for the aged under Social Security) and Medicaid, and the Supplementary Security Income program; the liberalization of the Old Age Insurance program; and finally, the passage of revenue sharing—all of these have changed the picture. The food stamp program provides coverage for the working poor and narrows the discrepancy between high and low benefit states in AFDC; Medicare and Medicaid reduce the burden of medical expenses on the aged and some of the other poor groups in society; the Supplementary Security Income program is a big step toward federalization of aid for the aged, blind, and disabled; and revenue sharing relieves state treasuries. Finally, in addition to these steps already taken, both the Administration and powerful figures in Congress are proposing major national health insurance programs for the entire population.

Those who support incrementalism add to their historical arguments in favor of this approach, the argument of political feasibility. Because of the legislative responses cited above and because of abatement in the growth of the AFDC program, there is no current political support for major changes in the income-tested transfer system. They also argue that because overall reform proposals contain provisions that will make some current beneficiaries worse off, adverse societal consequences in the form of unfulfilled expectations and reduced trust in the political process will result.

Supporters of the overhaul position argue that the correct question is not how far the income support system has come, but how far there is still to go to reach an effective, efficient system. Millions of those in poverty still receive nothing from our income-tested transfer programs. Those who receive aid frequently do so at the cost of a loss both in self-respect and in freedom to spend their income as they see fit. Moreover, the current multiprogram system is very expensive to administer and leads to cumulative benefit reduction rates that are too high for work incentive purposes and to horizontal inequities, in that some families receive benefits from several programs while other equally poor families receive few or no benefits. Finally, the current system is so complex that bureaucrats cannot administer it, the Congress cannot control it, and beneficiaries cannot understand it.

Thus, which strategy—basic overhaul or incrementalism—should be pursued depends on two different kinds of assessments. The first is an assessment of what kinds of changes are politically feasible. These political arguments will not be discussed in this overview essay. The second is an assessment of how well the current system of programs is performing and whether its major weaknesses are correctable within the existing framework.

Issues relating to the performance of and potential for improvement in the current system are discussed under the following five topics: adequacy of coverage, particularly regarding the working poor; work incentives; costs to program beneficiaries of coercion and stigma; inefficiencies and inequities; program and administrative costs.

Inadequate Coverage of the Working Poor

Since the middle of the 1960s, one of the most important criticisms of our income-tested transfer system was that it did not cover the working poor. The "working poor" are families headed by an ablebodied, non-aged male whose income is below what is considered an acceptable minimum level. Today, 40 percent of all poor people live in such families; in half of these families, the male head works *full time* all year round.[2]

Failure to cover the working poor has been criticized on three grounds. First, because the working poor constitute such a large proportion of the total number of poor people, transfer programs that do not cover the working poor obviously cannot eliminate poverty. Second, providing aid to one group of poor persons (such as female-headed families) but not to another equally poor group is inequitable. Third, the existence of this horizontal inequity between male-headed and female-headed families creates an incentive for the breakup of families.[3] Given these strong arguments for coverage of the working poor, why have they not been covered by cash transfer programs? What sort of support is now available to them?

WHY HAVE THE WORKING POOR NOT BEEN COVERED?

At least two reasons seem to explain the omission of the working poor from the system. The first reason is the fear that, if aided, large numbers of male heads of families would either reduce their work effort substantially or quit work entirely. As the HEW paper emphasizes, most of the empirical evidence suggests that reductions in the work effort of male heads would be quite small. Nevertheless, concern about work effort still persists (and will be discussed in detail in the next section). Conference participants seemed to agree that income transfers are preferable to other (noncash) alternatives for eliminating poverty among the working poor and that, given the recent evidence, concern about adverse work incentive effects does not warrant excluding the working poor from coverage by some kind of income support program. Differences remained, however, as to the optimal transfer program.

A second reason for noncoverage of the working poor is that reducing poverty has only recently become an explicit objective of public policy. Prior to the 1960s the principle objective of our income transfer system was to reduce economic insecurity. The idea was to replace a *normal* flow of earnings that, for some unavoidable reason, had been interrupted. If earnings were reduced because of retirement, there was Old Age Insurance; if because of disability, Disability Insurance; if because of the death of the breadwinner, Survivors Insurance; if because of unemployment, Unemployment Insurance. The three federal income-tested transfer programs that were established by the 1935 Social Security Act–Aid to the Aged, Aid to Dependent Children, and Aid to the Blind–were supposed to be small programs that would wither away as the social insurance system matured. It was as if poverty were viewed as just a special case of economic insecurity.

In the 1960s, however, it began to be understood that income insecurity was only one cause of economic hardship. Many poor people have not suffered a significant, sudden reduction in their normal earnings. They are poor because the capacity of the family head to earn income is less than that needed, in society's judgment, to provide a minimally acceptable standard of living. (This discovery of the working poor was due, at least in part, to the adoption of poverty elimination as an explicit objective of public policy in the 1964 Economic Opportunity Act, and, perhaps even more important, to the development and acceptance of an official government definition of poverty. Only after poverty was defined and measured was it possible to identify the large proportion of the poor who were "working poor.") Given the existence of the working poor, it is clear that poverty is neither identical with nor simply a special case of economic insecurity. Many who suffer a sudden reduction in their customary income flow are not poor; many who are poor are *at* their normal income level. If reducing income poverty is a social objective, even the elimination of income insecurity will not achieve it.

Moreover, if poverty is defined not in absolute terms but in relation to the income of others–that is, when it is based on a relative standard, as it has been over the long run in the past—poverty, including that among families with ablebodied male heads, will continue to exist. Even with economic growth and greater general prosperity,[4] the need for income transfer programs would not be likely to vanish.

TO WHAT EXTENT ARE THE WORKING POOR NOW COVERED?

Participants in the conference disagreed on the extent to which the working poor are currently covered by the existing income transfer system. This disagreement stemmed, at least in part, from the fact that adequacy of coverage was measured by some in terms of the number of persons eligible for a program; others measured it in terms of persons who actually receive benefits. Since 1971, as noted in the HEW paper, there have been uniform eligibility and payment levels in the food stamp program. The program is also universal; all low-income families, including the working poor, are eligible. And the program is generous. As of June 1974, a family of four with gross income up to about $7,350 a year will be eligible for benefits.[5] If the income of such a family is between $3,000 and $7,350, their potential benefits from the food stamp program will actually be more generous than their cash benefits would have been under the most recent version of the Family Assistance Plan.[6]

If coverage is measured by the number of persons actually receiving benefits, however, the picture changes. As of February 1974, for example, 39 million persons were entitled to food stamps but 26 million (about two-thirds) of them were not receiving such benefits.[7]

Whether coverage should be defined in terms of who is eligible for benefits or who actually receives them is not clear. In part, the answer depends on why the eligibles are not receiving benefits and on the prognostication for future participation. If, on the one hand, low participation rates are due to lack of information, a campaign to increase public awareness of the potential benefits may be an answer. The promotional campaign encouraging enrollment in Title B of the Old Age Health Insurance program is an encouraging first precedent. Even better is the current promotional campaign, conducted by the American Red Cross on a contract from the federal government, to encourage enrollment in the Supplementary Security Income program. (While our society is justifiably concerned about overpayments and fraud and willing to spend funds to prevent them, shouldn't it be equally concerned about the millions of individuals who are entitled to receive benefits but do not?) If, on the other hand, beneficiaries are not claiming benefits because of the stigma associated with applying for and then using food stamps, the problem is more difficult to resolve within the framework of the existing program. Thus, the reasons for gaps between eligibility and participation in income-tested transfer programs affect judgments about whether we need an overhaul of the current system or incremental changes to achieve adequate coverage of the working poor.

The Work Incentives Issue

In any discussion of transfer programs that aid individuals who are expected to work, the work incentives issue is a central concern. There is a general consensus in society that ablebodied, non-aged males are expected to work. There is an equally broad consensus that the blind, aged, and disabled are not expected to work. No such consensus exists on either side of the issue for ablebodied female heads of households.[8]

Government programs that involve groups that society expects to work should not function in a fashion that seriously reduces their incentive to earn in the market. Such discouragement can be expected to come either from high implicit tax rates on earnings or from the existence of a guaranteed minimum (in the absence of any other means of support) that approaches earnings levels prevailing in the relevant labor markets.

If one takes the position that the *only* cause for concern is the economic costs that would arise from a reduction in the labor supply of ablebodied males (reduced GNP and greater program costs) and if one is further convinced by the empirical evidence that the economic costs are likely to be very small, then the categorization of our current system that is designed to separate out those who are expected to work from those who are not, will appear to be unnecessary and wasteful. In this case, a single universal system is quite attractive. However, if one believes that violations of the work ethic rather than economic costs are the primary concern or if one is not convinced by the available empirical evidence that the economic costs resulting from reductions in labor supply induced by transfer programs would be small, then categorization per se will not appear to be so irrational. The question then becomes, How much and what kind of categorization is desirable?

The HEW document reviews the empirical evidence on the work incentive issue, and notes that although income transfer programs can be expected to reduce the labor supply of secondary workers—wives, for example—the labor supply of working age ablebodied males seems to be very insensitive to changes in transfer payment alternatives. This review was judged by the conference participants to be an accurate summary of the evidence and led to agreement that the economic cost of transfer payments for ablebodied males—in terms both of forgone output of goods and services and of increased program costs—would not be very great. The more responsive labor supply evidenced for secondary workers appeared not to be a major cause for concern—the labor they contribute in the marketplace is substantially less, and there is at least a partial consensus that the work they do in the home in place of market labor is socially valuable.

Moreover, as noted in the HEW report, the costs of work tests are large. In addition to the administrative costs discussed in the report, the costs to income transfer beneficiaries can be substantial—particularly if, as in the current AFDC program, there are no jobs available. In this case once a week or every other week beneficiaries must incur the child care and transportation costs required for their reporting to the employment service, though no job offers are being made.

Yet, as the document notes, the current income transfer program for which working-age ablebodied men are eligible—Unemployment Insurance, food stamps, and AFDC-UF—all have work tests. For some participants, the labor supply evidence referred to above indicated that these are unnecessary, given the fact that most ablebodied prime-age men work full time when they can find work. And if this is the case, the generally agreed-upon costs of a work test—administrative costs, but also costs in terms of human dignity—would seem not to be worth the gain.

Three points were brought up at the conference, however, that cast a complicating light on the work test issue. First, the concern to minimize the number of individuals who quit work as a result of a transfer program is not the same as the concern to minimize the economic costs of the reduction in work effort caused by the program. For example, if economic costs were the only concern, one would be indifferent between a 5 percent reduction in labor supply that resulted from all beneficiaries reducing their work by 5 percent and a 5 percent reduction that resulted from 5 percent of all beneficiaries quitting their jobs. Society, however, is not likely to be indifferent. If a transfer program induces many poor male family heads to reduce work from 50 to 40 hours a week or causes many wives or children in poor families to work less, public concern is not likely to be great. But if such a program induced many poor male family heads to stop work altogether, the public would almost certainly be quite disturbed.

If either a negative income tax or a refundable tax credit with a decent guarantee—payment to a family with no other income—and without a work test were enacted, a few ablebodied males would be certain to quit work for at least awhile and live off the guarantee. While the New Jersey Income Maintenance Experiment and other econometric research on labor supply suggest that the number of such individuals is likely to be small, only the most naive can believe that *no one* will do so. If Congress is aware of the substantial costs of administering work tests, the inclusion of these tests in existing legislation suggests that the benefits of preventing even a small number of violations of the work ethic are considered to exceed these costs.

Second, while current evidence does not lead to the expectation of a major labor force withdrawal if such legislation were enacted, there is no experience available on which a long-run prediction can be based. If there were no clear penalties for stopping work, over the long run social mores might change. If so, a national comprehensive transfer program without a work test could have a significant long-run effect on work behavior. (Neither a short-term experiment nor cross-sectional data can be used to ascertain if social mores would so change in the long run.)

Finally, if it is impossible to secure an income maintenance reform without some provision to guard against labor force withdrawal, explicit consideration should be given to alternative ways of ensuring that those society expects to work will not find it easy to quit when aided by an income support program.

The majority view in American society today seems to be that there is a public responsibility to provide a decent minimum standard of living for those not expected to work. A universal transfer system with a guarantee so low as to eliminate the possibility of labor force withdrawal would not provide adequately for those not expected to work. Such a system therefore would effectively be ruled out as an option. Among the remaining primary alternatives are administrative work tests and programs such as earnings supplements or wage rate subsidies in which benefits are only paid to workers. An intermediate alternative is a negative income tax with a very low guarantee for those expected to work.

All these alternatives involve categorization. If an administrative work test were adopted, those who are not expected to work would not be required to register for employment and accept a suitable job offer as a condition of receiving benefits. Similarly, the low or zero guarantee of a negative income tax, earnings supplement, or wage rate subsidy would be inadequate for those who are not expected to work. In either case, categorization—differential treatment for those who are and who are not expected to work—would be required.

Work tests and zero guarantees can be considered equally effective in preventing individuals from quitting work for long periods of time if we assume that, as the period without employment lengthens, the work test becomes stiffer and the individual is ultimately confronted with a choice of working for pay or receiving nothing. Whether low guarantees would be equally effective depends upon how low is low. The higher the guarantee, the greater the probability that people will be able to and want to live without earnings.

For shorter durations, however, a program with an administrative work test and a high guarantee is likely to be less effective than a program in which there are no benefits in the absence of work effort. Any work test is likely to contain some "suitable" employment provision preventing workers from having to accept employment in a job that is not suitable in terms of some definition of worker skill. Even if there were no such provision, individuals could behave so as to avoid job offers for a short time. Only a program, therefore, that ties benefits to working can completely prevent the receipt of benefits by nonworkers.

Work tests require the establishment of a bureaucracy to administer them over and above the bureaucracy required to administer payments. Low or zero guarantees do not require this additional bureaucracy. The administrative costs of the work test strategy are, therefore, higher. A work-related program, on the other hand, denies benefits to individuals who cannot find jobs. If the overwhelming majority of program beneficiaries are not likely to quit work voluntarily even for short periods, then the cost of preventing a few from quitting work by the use of a zero guarantee rather than a work test is to penalize the many unemployed beneficiaries who are out of work not because of the program but because they cannot find an appropriate job.[9] A guaranteed public employment program could accompany a work-conditioned transfer program to alleviate this problem, but in addition to the other problems of public employment programs discussed in the HEW report, the administrative costs of such programs would be high.[10]

Even if differential treatment of those who are and who are not expected to work is desirable because of concern about work incentives, the degree of categorization and the large number of programs that characterize the current system may not be desirable. While a universal negative income tax or tax credit plus a work test for those who were expected to work would involve a form of categorization, the degree and costs of this kind of categorization would be much less than the categorization in the current system. Thus whether such a basic overhaul of the system is desirable depends not only upon the work incentives issue but as well upon the issues discussed in the next four sections.

Inefficiencies and Inequities Arising From the Current Multiprogram System

The waste and inequity generated by the overlapping benefits and cumulative tax rates in the current system are generally agreed to be substantial. These are compounded by the confusions and lack of administrative control that are the inevitable results of inconsistent definitions of filing units, accounting periods, and criteria for eligibility. Nor are these problems limited to the income transfer system. They also extend into the positive tax system.

A simple income support system should have three desirable attributes. It should be understood both by the administrators and the beneficiaries, it should be designed to ensure that the intended effects are indeed the effects it has, and it should be subject to administrative control. The issue, then, is this: Given that the current system scores low on these criteria, can it be rationalized so as to come nearer to meeting them?

The HEW document suggests that rationalization is difficult. Aside from the political difficulties of trying to modify programs that have strong constituencies and are under the jurisdiction of 20 different Congressional committees, there are major practical problems. These inhere in the enormous inconsistencies in the primary elements of the existing transfer programs: the period for which income is counted in determining the transfer (the accounting period); who or what family group is the eligible party (the filing unit); the rate at which the benefits are reduced as income rises (the tax rate); and the definition of what income shall be counted. The four most important income-tested programs—SSI, AFDC, food stamps, and Medicaid—are inconsistent in all of these dimensions. If one adds to this the fact that some beneficiaries of these programs are also taxpayers in the positive tax scheme (with its own inconsistencies), the problem is compounded.

In addition to administrative rationality, an income support system should also have a benefit reduction rate low enough not to inhibit the desire to work, and it should produce the same benefit for two families who are equally poor. Certain combinations of current programs—both the document and conference participants emphasized—produce tax rates that are higher than the top marginal rate in the positive tax. In some cases the cumulated rates approach 100 percent, while in other cases there are "notches" so that total income actually decreases with an increase in earnings. They also produce a situation in which some families benefit from many programs, while others, equally poor, benefit from fewer or none.

These are serious problems. A replacement of existing programs with a single comprehensive program could relieve them. However, even if only medical insurance and day care programs were to be combined with a new simplified program these problems would not disappear. Nor would the horizontal inequity problem be solved without major reform of the positive tax system. In any case, it is not clear whether the elimination of notches and horizontal inequities in existing programs and the reduction in the cumulation of tax rates would be any more difficult to achieve politically or administratively within the current context than the substitution of one new comprehensive program for all the functioning old ones.

And there is a further cost of major simplification that some, in the final analysis, find unacceptable. The substitution of one universal program for the many current programs could substantially ameliorate horizontal inequities even if the positive tax system were to remain unreformed. But it would do so only at a cost. If benefit levels in the new universal program were set high enough to ensure that people currently receiving multiple benefits would not be made worse off, the program would be relatively expensive to taxpayers. But the Administration is not likely to propose, nor is Congress likely to pass, a program that leaves no beneficiary less well off. What is more likely is that a new universal program would provide more generous benefits to many of the poor—particularly the working poor—than they are now receiving, but less generous benefits than they are now receiving to other poor groups—particularly AFDC beneficiaries in the high benefit states. To some people, making any existing beneficiaries worse off is an unacceptable cost. To others, it is the unavoidable but acceptable cost of improving the system for the benefit of all.

Coercion and Stigma

Nonmonetary effects of the income transfer system on the people receiving the benefits constitute important considerations in judging alternative programs. Although not explicitly included in the HEW document, these criteria are implicit in the discussion of cash versus in-kind transfers and in the ranking of vouchers ahead of direct provision of goods and services. Two such effects to be discussed here are coercion and stigma.

The case for minimizing the coercive effect of a program on the expenditure decisions of beneficiaries rests on the belief that adults are the best judge of what is in their own interest. Conversely, the case for in-kind transfers rests primarily on either a desire to subsidize only certain kinds of beneficiary consumption (which implies a dislike of beneficiaries' consumption choices) or on political feasibility grounds arising out of an assessment as to the extent of public preferences for in-kind rather than cash transfers.

While in-kind programs constrain beneficiary choices, some may have rationales that override these coercion costs. For example, child care subsidies can be justified on the grounds of creating equity between one- and two-worker families (or zero- and one-worker families in the case of one-adult families). To the extent that child care is a cost incurred because of work, the argument goes, it should be deducted from income for the purpose of calculating either tax liability or benefit eligibility. This principle is now recognized in the positive federal income tax code. To the extent that child care grants only offset work expenses, however, they are not a subsidy as conventionally defined. Consequently, there is no case for income conditioning them and no problem of integrating child care with income-tested cash transfers. If AFDC mothers are required to work, however, there is a strong case for providing child care subsidies to them. This is where the current integration problem arises.

In-kind medical care subsidies appear to some to be justified on at least two grounds. Competent medical care is frequently essential to the quality of life and sometimes to life itself. As a consequence there is a consensus that no one should be denied medical care because they cannot afford it. In addition, medical expenses are very erratic. On occasion they can be high enough to entail financial catastrophe. Because the size of a medical bill constituting a financial catastrophe depends upon family income, it can be argued that the private market will not provide coverage that adequately protects low-income families against catastrophe.

To what extent are these justifications for child care and medical care subsidies convincing? Are there comparable justifications for food and housing subsidies? Those who favor the drastic overhaul approach see little justification for food subsidies as opposed to cash subsidy programs.[11] Those favoring an incremental approach stress the greater political support that such in-kind programs appear to be able to generate.

Stigma encompasses a second set of issues that concern the nonmonetary effect of a program on beneficiaries. The extent of stigma is judged by the degree to which the application for or receipt of aid from the program results in humiliation or loss of self-respect on the part of the beneficiary. Programs that aid only the poorer members of society have often been administered in such a way as to humiliate program beneficiaries. Throughout most of the history of the British Poor Law and its American descendant, this policy was deliberate.[12] The design was to discourage potential beneficiaries from applying for benefits by making the receipt of benefits a humiliating experience. While the current administration of income-tested programs is for the most part no longer characterized by such deliberate abuse, much abuse still exists. Moreover, so long as income tests are retained in our transfer programs, it is possible to return to the harsh practices of the past. Previous eras of relative benevolence have been followed by more stringent ones.

Even if income-tested programs are administered in the most benign way possible, beneficiaries must still declare themselves "poor" in order to receive aid. In our country, where so much stress is put on economic success and where the dominant ideology is that "with hard work anyone can make it," to admit to being poor is almost synonymous with an admission of failure. Indeed, the desire to avoid this labeling effect may be one of the reasons that so many of the working poor are not claiming the food stamps benefits to which they are entitled.[13]

The universal tax credit proposal, as the HEW document suggests, scores high on the avoidance of stigma. But how well it would score if it were enacted would depend in part on how the program were administered. If gross payments were paid out every month or week to everyone—rich and poor alike—there would clearly be no stigma because no one would have to declare himself poor to claim a benefit. However, if gross payments were not made to everyone it would score less well. If it were administered through IRS and the withholding system, there would exist no need on the part of those who are employed to apply for benefits; workers entitled to a supplement would have it added to their paychecks, while those who owed taxes would have them withheld from their paychecks.[14] Nonworkers, however, would still have to apply for and be subject to the stigma of declaring oneself poor.

At this time, however, a refundable tax credit may not be politically feasible. In consequence, incrementalists who believe this and who take the stigma issue seriously, advocate an expansion of the social insurance part of the current income transfer system rather than further extensions of the income-tested programs.

Whether or not expansion of the social insurance system is a desirable incremental strategy depends upon several factors. (1) How optimistic is the prognosis for minimizing the stigma attached to income-tested programs? (2) How much less target efficient an expansion of social insurance programs would be than alternative programs that are income-tested?[15] (3) How much importance is attached to the criteria of target efficiency and stigma?

Program Costs

One of the principal criticisms of the current system has been high and, until recently, rapidly rising costs in the AFDC program. Costs of programs have two components—transfer costs and administrative costs. Between 1960 and 1969 the cost of the AFDC program more than tripled (from $1 billion to $3.2 billion). By 1974, the cost of the AFDC program was $8 billion for more than 11 million beneficiaries. This dramatic increase in costs and caseloads during the 1960s was a principal source of dissatisfaction to liberals and conservatives alike. It is what most people meant when they spoke of a "welfare crisis."

One of the reasons that some people supported the Family Assistance Plan was that they believed that even though it would raise transfer costs and caseloads in the short run, it would reduce both in the long run. Similarly, one of the arguments used by some of those who now favor an overhaul approach is that passage of a single universal program—which would replace at least AFDC, AFDC-UF, and the food stamps programs, and forestall passage of a housing allowance and perhaps a work bonus—would be more expensive now but less expensive in the long run. In effect, "more" would be obtained for "less." Not everyone agrees that more can be obtained for less. Some legislators, who believe that too much is being spent on income transfer programs, also believe that the best way to reduce costs is to contract existing programs, rather than replace them by funding a new comprehensive one. Similarly, many who favor the complete overhaul approach do so precisely because they want to redistribute more, not less, income to the poorer members of our society.

"Welfare reform" throughout the 1960s and early 1970s has thus been fueled by two seemingly incompatible objectives: (1) to extend the income-tested transfer system to reduce poverty and (2) to reduce costs and caseloads. Because some of those who want to reduce costs believe the "more now means less later" argument while some of those who want to expand the system reject this argument, they can both support the same reform position. Thus differences over the validity of this hypothesis serve the useful political function of reconciling the differences in objectives for "welfare reform."

A multiprogram system with overlapping benefits compared with a single universal program may or may not increase the transfer cost component. There is no doubt at all, however, that the administrative cost component increases dramatically with both the degree of administrative discretion and the proliferation of separate programs. The administrative costs of the Institute for Research on Poverty's recently completed urban and rural negative income tax experiments are substantially less per family than those in the AFDC program. For a program that covered all families and unrelated individuals below 150 percent of the poverty level, such differences in administration would lead to differences in cost of about $3 billion. Moreover, the difference in administrative costs would be even larger if one compared the cost of administering all the present programs *plus* a negative income tax for the working poor alone, to the cost of a straight cash transfer (say, a universal negative income tax) to all families.

Conclusion

The HEW paper discusses the major shortcomings of our current income-tested transfer programs, identifies most of the major issues in income transfer reform, and analyzes most of the trade-offs among competing objectives.[16] At the conference, the paper was discussed in the context of the question, How can the current income-tested transfer system be changed in order to enhance its effectiveness in raising the incomes of the poorer members of our society; reduce the budget coercive and demeaning aspects of the current system; and reduce the high cumulative benefit reduction rates, horizontal inequities, administrative duplications, and other inefficiencies that arise out of the staggering complexity of our current multiprogram system? While conference participants agreed that changes to achieve these objectives were important, there was substantial disagreement about the best way to achieve these objectives. Some participants argued for a complete overhaul of the system; others argued for an incremental reform approach. Moreover, those who took the same side on this issue frequently did so for different reasons.

Such disagreement is not surprising, for the criteria for evaluating alternative income transfer programs conflict. What the HEW report does so well is to identify these conflicts and the consequent trade-offs among the alternatives. This kind of analysis is an essential input into sound decision-making. Hopefully, the HEW report and this essay will contribute to an informed debate about how to strengthen our income support system.

Notes to Part Two

1. An example of the incremental approach was favored by one participant who suggested adding to our current system a work bonus and a housing allowance and/or Unemployment Insurance reforms to cover more of the working poor, and possibly cashing out food stamps. In addition, he favored establishing a federal minimum payment for AFDC, requiring all states to adopt AFDC-UF, and establishing the same definitions of eligibility units, income, and accounting periods.

2. Whereas the family is the appropriate unit for calculating administrative costs, data on individuals are more appropriate in appraising the poverty-reducing impact of various transfer programs. Thus, although the HEW paper notes that 27 percent of all poor families are headed by ablebodied males, 40 percent of all poor persons are in families headed by a male under 65. One conference participant argued that if money incomes were deflated for cost of living differentials, the proportion of poor persons who are in working poor families would be much smaller than 40 percent. While most other conference participants doubted that this would be so, the question is a researchable one.

3. No reliable empirical evidence on the magnitude of this effect exists. Even if an ideal universal program were in place—one that did not provide more generous aid to female-headed than to intact families, as the current system does—there would probably be more family breakups than if there were no program at all. Although good evidence is not available, it is reasonable to believe that financial security provides the freedom to dissolve marriages that are unsuccessful or to avoid seeking marriage or remarriage for economic support reasons. How one appraises the desirability or undesirability of such an effect depends upon one's values regarding the maintenance of "intact families" per se as opposed to providing men and women the freedom to make marital choices on grounds other than economic necessity.

4. When income transfers are considered, the objectives of reducing poverty and inequality are closely related. At any point in time, the use of income transfers to reduce poverty necessarily involves an increase in the share of income going to the poorest members of society and a decrease in the share going to everyone else. Thus, reducing poverty through income transfers by its very nature involves a redistribution of income. Moreover, to the extent that poverty is a relative phenomenon—that is, the extent to which an individual both feels poor and is considered by others to be poor depends upon how low his income is in relation to the general standard of living in his society—the distinction between reducing poverty and reducing inequality becomes even less clear.

Viewed in this way the choice between a negative income tax that targets most of its benefits on the poor and either a more generous negative income tax or refundable tax credit that is much less target efficient depends not so much on whether the goal is to reduce poverty or inequality but rather on the degree to which priority is assigned to the goal of reducing inequality.

5. In the food stamp program, the eligibility level of income is determined after deductions for work-related expenses, including the Social Security payroll tax and the income tax. There is, however, an assets test in the program that excludes some low-income families from eligibility.

6. Conversely, for families of four with incomes below $3,000, potential benefits will be less generous than the most recent version of FAP.

7. These estimates were developed by the staff of the Subcommittee on Fiscal Policy of the Joint Economic Committee, chaired by Representative Martha Griffiths. Barbara Bolland estimates that in 1967 only 56 percent of those eligible for AFDC actually received benefits. About 800,000 families who were eligible did not receive any benefits. According to her estimates a substantial share of the increase in the number of AFDC beneficiaries between 1967 and 1970 is attributable to the increase in participation rates—from 56 percent in 1967 to 78 percent in 1970. See Barbara Boland, in Joint Economic Committee, Subcommittee on Fiscal Policy, *Studies in Public Welfare,* "Participation in the Aid to Families with Dependent Children Program," Paper No. 12 (Part I)(Washington, D.C.: U.S. Government Printing Office, November 4, 1973).

8. When the AFDC program was established, the general view was that a woman's place was in the home. One avowed purpose of the program was to substitute benefits for the earnings of the missing husband so that the mother could devote her time to raising her children. One of the reasons that the AFDC program has become controversial is because attitudes toward the appropriate role of women have begun to change. Until some new consensus is reached on whether female heads of households are or are not expected to work, AFDC will remain controversial.

9. A mitigating factor in this case is the Unemployment Insurance system. Although UI caters quite well to people in covered employment with a regular job history, it will not in the absence of a major reform handle the unemployed who have never been able to be regularly employed or the many who work at jobs that are as yet uncovered by unemployment compensation.

10. Because a wage rate subsidy places a negative benefit reduction rate on earnings, it could be used to reduce the cumulative benefit reduction rate problem. An earnings supplement has a negative benefit reduction rate on low earnings and a positive tax rate (as in an NIT or tax credit) on higher earnings. Because most beneficiaries have earnings in the higher range, the earnings supplement is not as advantageous on this score as the wage rate subsidy.

11. While the HEW report appears to lean in the direction of cashing out food stamps, there also appears to be a great deal of sympathy for a housing allowance. The kind of housing allowance the authors have in mind, however, is really a cash grant, which is related to housing only insofar as the amount is determined by local housing costs.

12. See Karl de Schweinitz, *England's Road to Social Security* (Philadelphia: University of Pennsylvania Press, 1943); Samuel Mencher, *Poor Law to Poverty Program: Economic Security Policy in Britain and the United States* (Pittsburgh: University of Pittsburgh Press, 1967).

13. On the other hand, some programs with income tests appear not to discourage beneficiaries because of stigma, although how well these examples generalize is questionable. Many college scholarships, for example, are awarded on the basis of need, and there is an earnings test in the Old Age Insurance program. But getting an education is a highly valued social activity, and the earnings test in the OAI program is not an income but a degree-of-retirement test.

14. In this connection, although not mentioned in the document, an earnings supplement could be administered in the same way. Of course, if earnings fluctuate during the year, there would be under- and over-payments in an earnings supplement that would have to be reconciled on an annual basis—presumably through the income tax.

15. Although the HEW report asserts that expansion of social insurance programs are less target efficient than income-tested programs, it presents no estimates of how much less target efficient particular proposals for expansion of the social insurance program would be than particular proposals for income-tested programs. The target efficiency of particular proposals will vary dramatically—even if all the proposals are of the same type—a negative income tax, for example.

16. One major omission from the HEW report in terms of analyzing the trade-offs is an emphasis on the fact that informed decision-making requires a solid base of empirical evidence in addition to a firm understanding of theoretical issues and a set of well-delineated, widely accepted criteria. The choice among various programs, as argued above, depends on the costs of the alternatives. Moreover, an accurate understanding of the characteristics of the poor is essential to resolving the most elemental issues of policy strategy. The choice between a wage rate subsidy and a negative income tax or tax credit, for example, rests in part on whether poverty is principally due to low wages or to unemployment. A negative income tax or tax credit would aid both groups, whereas a wage subsidy would not aid those with relatively adequate wage rates who are poor because of unemployment. Similarly, the choice

between a universal program and various categorical programs rests in part on how stable is the composition of the various groups of the poor. The more they vary over time, the more costly, inefficient, and inequitable categorical programs became. In the absence of data on such questions, informed policy-making is impossible. In this sense then, the HEW report cannot-and was not designed to—stand alone.

Bibliography

Institute for Research on Poverty Publications Related to Welfare Policy Reform*

DISCUSSION PAPERS

52-69 *Impact of a Negative Income Tax on the Number of Substandard Housing Units*
Hugh O. Nourse

53-69 *Income Maintenance and the State and Local Tax-Expenditure Package*
A. James Heins

54-69 *A Base for the Negative Income Tax*
Charles W. Meyer

57-69 *Nixon's Family Assistance Plan*
Robert J. Lampman

*Single copies of most publications are available without charge by writing to the Institute for Research on Poverty, University of Wisconsin, 4315 Social Science Building, 1180 Observatory Drive, Madison, Wisconsin 53706. Institute Monographs are available for purchase from Academic Press, 111 Fifth Avenue, New York, New York 10003.

65-70 *The New Jersey-Pennsylvania Experiment: A Field Study in Negative Taxation*
David Elesh, Jack Ladinsky, Myron J. Lefcowitz, and Seymour Spilerman

69-70 *Adjusted and Extended Preliminary Results from the Urban Graduated Work Incentive Experiment*
Harold W. Watts

82-70 *On the Stigma Effect and the Demand for Welfare Programs: A Theoretical Note*
Burton A. Weisbrod

83-70 *Poverty Theories and Income Maintenance: Validity and Policy Relevance*
David Elesh

90-71 *The Work and Human Investment Incentives of Negative Income Tax and Wage Subsidy Programs*
Irwin Garfinkel

96-71 *Participant Demand Functions for In-Kind Transfer Payments*
W. Keith Bryant

98-71 *Mid-Experiment Report on Basic Labor-Supply Response*
Harold W. Watts

101-71 *On Estimating the Labor Supply Effects of a Negative Income Tax*
Irwin Garfinkel

105-71 *The Welfare Reform Provisions in H.R. 1*
Robert J. Lampman

106-71 *After 15 Months: Preliminary Results from the Urban Negative Income Tax Experiment*
David Elesh, Jack Ladinsky, Myron J. Lefcowitz, and Arnold Shore

111-72 *The Definition of "Income" Under a Negative Income Tax*
William A. Klein

117-72 *The Effect of Income Maintenance Laws on Fertility in the United States*
Glen G. Cain

118-72 *Appendices to Income Maintenance Laws and Fertility in the United States*
Glen G. Cain

133-72 *Welfare Policy and the Employment Rate of AFDC Mothers*
Irwin Garfinkel and Larry L. Orr

137-72 *The Evaluation by Recipients of In-Kind Transfers*
Maria Schmundt, Eugene Smolensky, and Leanna Stiefel

145-72 *Social-Psychological Effects on Labor Supply in the New Jersey-Pennsylvania Experiment*
Sonia Wright

147-72 *Labor Force Participation Among Male Heads of Household in the New Jersey-Pennsylvania Negative Income Tax Experiment: Preliminary Results*
David Elesh and Kevin McCarthy

150-72 *Interpreting the Results of Short-Duration Income-Maintenance Experiments: An Investigation of Biases in Predicting Long-Run Behavior*
Charles E. Metcalf and Glen G. Cain

154-73 *Social Accounting for Transfers*
Robert J. Lampman

161-73 *The Politics of Poor Relief: A Study in Ambiguities*
Matthew Holden, Jr.

165-73 *Estimates of Tax Rates in the AFDC Program*
Irene Lurie

166-73 *On Comparison of Income Distribution Plans*
Harold W. Watts and Jon K. Peck

175-73 *Earnings Supplementation Plans for "Working Poor" Families: An Evaluation of Alternatives*
Robert Haveman, Irene Lurie, and Thad Mirer

180-73 *What Does It Do For the Poor? A New Test for National Policy*
Robert J. Lampman

185-73 *Alternative Definitions of Income Redistribution*
Jean Behrens and Eugene Smolensky

186-73 *When Do Recipients Value Transfers at their Cost to Taxpayers*
Maria Schmundt, Eugene Smolensky, Leanna Stiefel

202-74 *Income Maintenance and Welfare Reform: Papers and Comments*
Robert J. Lampman, James Tobin, Alice M. Rivlin, and Alvin L. Schorr

REPRINTS

1. *Some Basic Problems of Negative Income Taxation*
William A. Klein, 1966

3. *Ends and Means in the War Against Poverty*
Robert J. Lampman, 1966

6. *How Much Does the American System of Transfers Benefit the Poor?*
Robert J. Lampman, 1967

10. *Schemes for Transferring Income to the Poor*
Christopher Green and Robert J. Lampman, 1967

24. *Negative Taxes and the Poverty Problem–A Review Article*
Peter A. Diamond, 1968

25. *Formulas for Income Maintenance: Their Distributional Impact*
Martin David and Jane Leuthold, 1968

39. *Graduated Work Incentives: An Experiment in Negative Taxation*
Harold W. Watts, 1969

49. *Transfer and Redistribution as Social Process*
Robert J. Lampman, 1970

52. *A Model Negative Income Tax Statute*
James G. Speth, Jr., et al., 1970

54. *Field Experimentation in Income Maintenance*
Harold Watts, John Conlisk, D. Lee Bawden, and Larry L. Orr, 1970

56. *Partial Benefit Schedules in Unemployment Insurance: Their Effect on Work Incentive*
Raymond Munts, 1970

58. *Farm Operators Under the Negative Income Tax*
Charles W. Meyer and William E. Saupe, 1970

60. *Work, Welfare, and the Nixon Reform Proposals*
Joel Handler and Ellen Jane Hollingsworth, 1970

61. *Transfer Approaches to Distribution Policy*
Robert J. Lampman, 1970

64. *Income Maintenance and the Rural Poor: An Experimental Approach*
D. Lee Bawden, 1970

66. *Reforming Welfare: The Constraints of the Bureaucracy and the Clients*
Joel Handler and Ellen Jane Hollingsworth, 1971

67. *The Negative Income Tax: Accounting Problems and a Proposed Solution*
Michael R. Asimow and William A. Klein, 1971

71. *Familial Relationships and Economic Well-Being: Family Unit Rules for a Negative Income Tax*
William Klein, 1971

72. *Family Assistance Plan: An Analysis and Evaluation*
D. Lee Bawden, Glen Cain, Leonard J. Hausman, 1971

73. *Current Status of Income Maintenance Experiments:*
"The Graduated Work Incentives Experiment: Current Progress" by Harold W. Watts;
"The Seattle Experiment: The Combined Effect of Income Maintenance and Manpower Investments" by Mordecai Kurz and Robert G. Spiegelman;
"The Gary Income Maintenance Experiment: Plans and Progress" by Terence F. Kelly and Leslie Singer;
"Discussion" by James N. Morgan, 1971

74. *On Comparing Income Maintenance Alternatives*
Theodore R. Marmor, 1971

78. *Work Incentives and Welfare Reform: The FAP Experience*
Robert F. Smith and W. Joseph Heffernan, 1972

92. *Federal-State Interests in Welfare Administration*
Joel F. Handler, 1973

93. *Legislative, Administrative, and Judicial Changes in the AFDC Program, 1967-71*
Irene Lurie, 1973

94. *Variations in Negative Tax Rates in Current Public Assistance Programs: An Example of Administrative Discretion*
W. Joseph Heffernan, 1973

99. *Is In-Kind Redistribution Efficient?*
Irwin Garfinkel, 1973

100. *Cost and Distributional Implications of a Credit Income Tax Plan*
Russell Lidman, 1973

105. *Public and Private Transfers as Social Process*
Robert J. Lampman, 1973

108. *A Skeptical Note on "The Optimality" of Wage Subsidy Programs*
Irwin Garfinkel, 1973

110. *Making Inferences from Controlled Income Maintenance Experiments*
Charles E. Metcalf, 1973

112. *Work-Conditioned Subsidies As an Income-Maintenance Strategy: Issues of Program Structure and Integration*
Robert H. Haveman, 1974

MONOGRAPHS

The "Deserving Poor": A Study in Welfare Administration
Joel F. Handler and Ellen Jane Hollingsworth. 1971
$10.50

Ends and Means of Reducing Income Poverty
Robert J. Lampman. 1971
$8.95 hardcover, $3.95 paper

Income Maintenance: Interdisciplinary Approaches to Research
Larry L. Orr, Robinson G. Hollister, and Myron J. Lefcowitz, editors, with the assistance of Karen Hester. 1971
$10.50

Income Maintenance and Labor Supply: Econometric Studies
Glen G. Cain and Harold W. Watts, editors. 1973
$15.00

The Coercive Social Worker: British Lessons for American Social Services
Joel F. Handler. 1973
$5.95

BIBLIOGRAPHIES

Income Support Schemes: bibliography and annotations to academic literature including references to newspaper citations (272 p.)
Colin Cameron, 1972

Attitudes of the Poor and Attitudes Toward the Poor: bibliography with selected annotations (approximately 250 p.)
Colin Cameron, forthcoming 1974

OTHER PUBLICATIONS

The Journal of Human Resources: Education, Manpower, and Welfare Policies, Glen G. Cain, editor; Barbara D. Dennis, managing editor. Published four times a year by the University of Wisconsin Press under the auspices of the Industrial Relations Research Institute, the Health Economics Research Center, and the Institute for Research on Poverty.

Subscriptions are $10.00 per year for individuals and $20.00 per year for institutions and are available from University of Wisconsin Press, Box 1379, Madison, Wisconsin 53701.

General Publications Related to Welfare Policy Reform

Aaron, Henry J. *Why is Welfare So Hard to Reform?* Washington, D.C.: The Brookings Institution, 1973.

———. *Shelter and Subsidies: Who Benefits from Federal Housing Policies?* Washington, D.C.: The Brookings Institution, 1972.

Bawden, D. Lee; Cain, Glen G.; and Hausman, Leonard J. "The Family Assistance Plan: An Analysis and Evaluation," *Public Policy* (Spring 1971): 323-53.

Breul, Frank R. "Work and Welfare Do Not Mix," *Social Service Review* 47 (March 1973): 93-95.

Browning, Edgar K. "Alternative Programs for Income Redistribution: The NIT and the NWT," 63 *American Economic Review* 1 (1973): 38-49.

Burns, Eveline, ed. *Children's Allowance and the Economic Welfare of Children: The Report of a Conference.* New York: Citizen's Committee for the Children of New York, 1968.

———. *Social Security and Public Policy.* New York: McGraw-Hill, 1956.

Esterly, Stanley, and Esterly, Glenn. *Freedom From Dependence: Welfare Reform as a Solution to Poverty.* Washington, D.C.: Public Affairs Press, 1971.

Fried, Edward R., et al. *Setting National Priorities: The 1974 Budget.* Washington, D.C.: The Brookings Institution, 1973.

Friedman, Milton. *Capitalism and Freedom.* Chicago: University of Chicago Press, 1962.

Glennerster, Howard. "A Tax Credit Scheme for Britain?–A Review of the British Government's Green Paper," 8 *The Journal of Human Resources* 4 (Fall 1973): 422-35.

Goodwin, Leonard. *Do the Poor Want to Work?* Washington, D.C.: The Brookings Institution, 1972.

Green, Christopher. *Negative Taxes and the Poverty Problem.* Washington, D.C.: The Brookings Institution, 1972.

Handler, Joel F. *Reforming the Poor: Welfare Policy, Federalism, and Morality.* New York: Basic Books, 1972.

Hildebrand, George. *Poverty, Income Maintenance, and the Negative Income Tax.* Ithaca, N.Y.: New York State School of Labor Relations, Cornell University, 1967.

Journal of Human Resources, The. Volume 8, Supplement (1973). Seven articles on work and welfare.

Kershaw, David N., and Lindheim, Barbara Levitz. *Administrative Issues in Planning and Implementing Welfare Reform Proposals.* Princeton, N.J.: Mathematica, Inc., 1973.

Kershaw, Joseph. *Government Against Poverty.* Chicago: Markham, 1970.

Komisar, Lucy. *Down and Out in the U.S.A.: A History of Social Welfare.* New York: Grolier, Inc., 1973.

Levitan, Sar A.; Rein, Martin; and Marwick, David. *Work and Welfare Go Together.* Baltimore: Johns Hopkins University Press, 1972.

Lurie, Irene, ed. *Integrating Income Maintenance Programs.* New York: Academic Press, forthcoming.

Marmor, Theodore R., ed. *Poverty Policy: A Compendium of Cash Transfer Proposals.* Chicago: Aldine-Atherton, Inc., 1971.

Marris, Peter, and Rein, Martin. *Dilemmas of Social Reform: Poverty and Community Action in the United States.* London: Routledge and Kegan Paul, 1967.

Moynihan, Daniel P. *The Politics of a Guaranteed Income: The Nixon Administration and the Family Assistance Plan.* New York: Random House, 1973.

______, ed. *On Understanding Poverty: Perspectives from the Social Sciences.* New York: Basic Books, 1969.

Pechman, Joseph A.; Aaron, Henry J.; and Taussig, Michael K. *Social Security, Perspectives for Reform.* Washington, D.C.: The Brookings Institution, 1968.

Piven, Frances Fox, and Cloward, Richard A. *Regulating the Poor: The Functions of Public Welfare.* New York: Pantheon Books, 1971.

President's Commission on Income Maintenance Programs. *Poverty Amid Plenty: The American Paradox. Technical Studies. Background Papers.* Washington, D.C.: U.S. Government Printing Office, 1969.

Proposals for a Tax-Credit System. Cmnd. 5116. London: HMSO, October 1972.

Schorr, Alvin L. *Explorations in Social Policy.* New York: Basic Books, 1968.

Schultze, Charles, et al. *Setting National Priorities: The 1973 Budget.* Washington, D.C.: The Brookings Institution, 1972.

Steiner, Gilbert Y. *Social Insecurity: The Politics of Welfare.* Chicago: Rand McNally and Co., 1966.

———. *The State of Welfare.* Washington, D.C.: The Brookings Institution, 1971.

Tobin, James. "Raising the Incomes of the Poor," in *Agenda for the Nation,* Kermit Gordon, ed. Washington, D.C.: The Brookings Institution, 1968.

———, and Wallis, W. Allen. *Welfare Programs: An Economic Appraisal.* Washington, D.C.: American Enterprise Institute for Public Policy Research, 1968.

U.S. Advisory Council on Public Welfare. *Having the Power, We Have the Duty.* Washington, D.C.: U.S. Government Printing Office, 1966.

U.S. Congress. Joint Economic Committee. Subcommittee on Fiscal Policy. *Studies in Public Welfare.* Washington, D.C.: U.S. Government Printing Office, 1972-74.

Paper No. 1. "Public Income Transfer Programs: The Incidence of Multiple Benefits and the Issues Raised by Their Receipt," April 10, 1972.
Paper No. 2. "Handbook of Public Income Transfer Programs," October 16, 1972.
Paper No. 3. "The Effectiveness of Manpower Training Programs: A Review of Research on the Impact on the Poor," November 20, 1972.
Paper No. 4. "Income Transfer Programs: How They Tax the Poor," December 22, 1972.
Paper No. 5. Issues in Welfare Administration:
(Part 1) "Welfare–An Administrative Nightmare," December 31, 1972.
(Part 2) "Intergovernmental Relationships," March 12, 1973.
(Part 3) "Implications of the Income Maintenance Experiments," March 12, 1973.
Paper No. 6. "How Public Benefits Are Distributed in Low-Income Areas," March 26, 1973. Additional Material for Paper No. 6: "How Public Welfare Benefits Are Distributed in Low-Income Areas," August 6, 1973.
Paper No. 7. "Issues in the Coordination of Public Welfare Programs," July 2, 1973.

Paper No. 8. "Income-Tested Social Benefits in New York: Adequacy, Incentives, and Equity," July 8, 1973.

Paper No. 9 (Part 1). "Concepts in Welfare Program Design," August 20, 1973.

Paper No. 10. "The New Supplemental Security Income Program–Impact on Current Benefits and Unresolved Issues," October 7, 1973.

Paper No. 11. "The Labor Market Impacts of the Private Retirement System," October 30, 1973.

Paper No. 12. The Family, Poverty, and Welfare Programs:

(Part I) "Factors Influencing Family Instability," November 4, 1973.

(Part II) "Household Patterns and Government Policies," December 3, 1973.

Paper No. 13. "How Income Supplements Can Affect Work Behavior," February 18, 1974.

Paper No. 14. "Public Welfare and Work Incentives: Theory and Practice," April 15, 1974.

U.S. Department of Health, Education, and Welfare. *Summary Report: New Jersey Graduated Work Incentive Experiment,* December 1973.

Zeckhauser, Richard, and Schuck, Peter. "An Alternative to the Nixon Income Maintenance Plan," *Public Interest* 19 (Spring 1970): 120-30.

Participants

Conference on Welfare Reform

Michael C. Barth—Director of Income Security Policy/Analysis, Office of the Assistant Secretary for Planning and Evaluation, Office of the Secretary, Department of Health, Education, and Welfare.

D. Lee Bawden—Fellow, Institute for Research on Poverty; Professor of Economics and Agricultural Economics, University of Wisconsin-Madison.

Glen G. Cain—Fellow, Institute for Research on Poverty; Professor of Economics, University of Wisconsin-Madison.

George J. Carcagno—Vice President of Urban Opinion Surveys Division, Mathematica, Inc.

Milton Friedman—The Paul Snowden Russell Distinguished Service Professor in the Department of Economics, University of Chicago.

Irwin Garfinkel—Staff Member, Institute for Research on Poverty; Associate Professor of Social Work, University of Wisconsin-Madison.

Joel F. Handler—Fellow, Institute for Research on Poverty; Professor of Law, University of Wisconsin-Madison.

Robert H. Haveman—Director and Fellow, Institute for Research on Poverty; Professor of Economics, University of Wisconsin-Madison.

Joseph Heffernan—Staff Member, Institute for Research on Poverty; Professor of Social Work, University of Wisconsin—Madison.

Robinson Hollister—Associate Professor of Economics, Swarthmore College.

Jack Ladinsky—Associate Director for Research and Fellow, Institute for Research on Poverty; Professor of Sociology, University of Wisconsin-Madison.

Irene Lurie—Assistant Professor of Economics, Union College.

Ida C. Merriam—Former Director of Research, Social Security Administration.

Charles E. Metcalf—Staff Member, Institute for Research on Poverty; Associate Professor of Economics, University of Wisconsin-Madison.

William A. Morrill—Assistant Secretary for Planning and Evaluation, Office of the Secretary, Department of Health, Education, and Welfare.

Richard Nathan—Senior Fellow, The Brookings Institution.

John L. Palmer—Director of Income Security Policy, Office of the Assistant Secretary for Planning and Evaluation, Office of the Secretary, Department of Health, Education, and Welfare.

Gilbert Y. Steiner—Director of Governmental Studies Program, The Brookings Institution.

John Todd—Brookings Institution Economic Policy Fellow; Assistant Professor of Economics, Williams College (on leave).

Alair Townsend—Director of Research, Subcommittee on Fiscal Policy of the Joint Economic Committee, United States Congress.

Index

Aaron Plan, 78-82
Aid to Families with Dependent Children (AFDC): adequacy of benefits, 97; administration of, 16-17; coverage in, 92-110; and earnings supplement program, 96-97; and integration with other programs, 103-04; and needs standard in, 17; and reasons for discontinuing cases in, 76; and refining present system, 97-110; and social insurance, 103-04; standardization of, 99-100; state payment standards in, 17; state supplementation of, 93-96; variability in program clientele in, 45-46; and welfare reform, 93-97; work limitations in, 16, 102; and unemployed fathers (AFDC-UF), 33, 34, 37, 57, 64, 88, 98, 102, 124, 167; and work incentives, 101-03; work requirements in, 19

Benefit reduction rate, 18, 34, 35, 61, 137
Breakeven level, 54, 101, 107, 135, 145
British Tax Credit Plan, 57, 75-77

California Work Experience project (CWEP), 81-82
Cash transfers, 48, 51-59. *See also* Transfer programs; Welfare system
Children's allowance, 56

Day care, 18, 66, 68, 77, 192

Earnings supplement, 73-75, 88, 96-97
Economic Opportunity Act (1964), 154
Emergency assistance, 24. *See also* General Assistance
Emergency Employment Act (1971), 81
Employment policy and the welfare system, 10-12

Family Assistance Plan (FAP), 20, 56, 60, 88, 92, 95, 122, 128, 141, 165
Federal-state relations in AFDC, 105-06
Food stamps, 19-20, 38, 89, 117, 133, 168

General Accounting Office (GAO), 33, 139
General Assistance, 24, 32, 89

H.R. 1, 73, 75, 77, 81, 116, 143
Housing assistance programs, 22-23
Housing Task Force, 138

Income stability in low-income population, 42-45
Income support system. *See* Transfer programs; Welfare system
Income-tested programs: technical characteristics of, 133-36. *See also* Welfare system
In-kind programs, 35-36, 58, 89-91, 119-20, 163
Intact families, coverage of, 85-91

Joint Economic Committee, Subcommittee on Fiscal Policy, 5, 37

Medicaid, 20-22
Mega Plan, 77-78, 87-88, 141
Michigan Survey Research Center, 24, 42-43, 138

Negative income tax plans, 54-55, 75-78
New Jersey Income Maintenance Experiment, 61, 63, 158, 165
Nixon, Richard M., 5
Notches in the welfare system, 22, 34, 101-02

Opportunities for Families Program (OFP), 56, 67, 68, 88

Payroll tax relief, 83-84, 88
Poverty, incidence of, in U.S., 24-31, 43
Public assistance. *See* Aid to Families with Dependent Children; Welfare system
Public employment, 67-68, 78-82

Quality Control System, 38, 104, 139

Reform in welfare system. *See* Welfare reform
Refundable tax credit. See Universal refundable tax credit

Social and private insurance system, 12-13, 85, 103-04
Social Security, 83-84
Social Security Act (1935), 154
Social transfer account. *See* Transfer system
State Employment Service, 19

Stigma in welfare, 162-64
Supplemental Security Income (SSI), 23-24, 32, 95, 103, 155

Talmadge amendment (1972), 57
Taxes, positive and negative, 52-53. *See also* Negative income tax plans
Transfer system: adequacy of, 27-30; coverage of, by family type, 24-31; cash and in-kind benefits of, 47-50; income-tested programs in, 112-22; problems of, 126

Universal refundable tax credit, 53-54, 59, 87-89, 158, 164

Vouchers, 35, 48-49, 113-14, 127. *See also* In-kind benefits
Wage rate subsidy, 69, 72-73, 84, 88
Welfare reform, 97-110, 126-29, 151-53
Welfare system: adequacy in, 40; administrative efficiency in, 36-38, 40; categorization in, 32-34; characteristics of, 31-39, 114-15; coherency and control in, 42; components of, 14-24; failure of, 124-26; family stability incentives in, 41; geographic differences in, 31-32; goals of, 39; horizontal equity in, 40; independence from, 41-42; inequities in, 160-62; integration techniques in, 116-22; program costs in, 164-66; stigma in, 162-64; target efficiency in, 38-40; vertical equity in, 41. *See also* Aid to Families with Dependent Children; Transfer system
Work-conditioned programs, 65, 71-84, 88-89, 130
Work disincentives, 34-35
Work incentives, 41, 61-65, 87-88, 156-60
Work Incentives Program (WIN), 19, 56, 57, 60, 63, 64, 84, 103
Work relief. *See* Public employment
Work requirements, 56, 60-70, 102-03
Working poor, coverage of, 153-56

5000-3L40085-74